DEVIL'S ADVOCATES

T0341707

DEVIL'S ADVOCATES is a series of books devoted to exploring the classics of horror cinema. Contributors to the series come from the fields of teaching, academia, journalism and fiction, but all have one thing in common: a passion for the horror film and a desire to share it with the widest possible audience.

'The admirable Devil's Advocates series is not only essential – and fun – reading for the serious horror fan but should be set texts on any genre course.'
Dr Ian Hunter, Reader in Film Studies, De Montfort University, Leicester

'Auteur Publishing's new Devil's Advocates critiques on individual titles... offer bracingly fresh perspectives from passionate writers. The series will perfectly complement the BFI archive volumes.' **Christopher Fowler, *Independent on Sunday***

'Devil's Advocates has proven itself more than capable of producing impassioned, intelligent analyses of genre cinema... quickly becoming the go-to guys for intelligent, easily digestible film criticism.' *Horror Talk.com*

'Auteur Publishing continue the good work of giving serious critical attention to significant horror films.' ***Black Static***

 DevilsAdvocatesbooks

 DevilsAdBooks

ALSO AVAILABLE IN THIS SERIES

FORTHCOMING

DEVIL'S ADVOCATES

THE BLAIR WITCH PROJECT

PETER TURNER

Acknowledgments

For my parents who let me grow up on a strict diet of horror, and for my wife (and Final Girl) Beth who admirably tries her best to withstand all the horror I can throw at her. Special thanks to Beth and her family, and to my own sisters, Emma and Helen, for their constant support and encouragement. Thanks also to John Atkinson at Auteur for believing I could do it, to Dr Paolo Russo for his guidance and to Ian Cooper for being a great teacher at the beginning of my Film Studies journey.

First published in 2014 by
Auteur, 24 Hartwell Crescent, Leighton Buzzard LU7 1NP
www.auteur.co.uk
Copyright © Auteur 2014

Series design: Nikki Hamlett at Cassels Design
Set by Cassels Design www.casselsdesign.co.uk
Printed and bound by CPI Group (UK) Ltd, Croydon, CR0 4YY

All rights reserved. No part of this publication may be reproduced in any material form (including photocopying or storing in any medium by electronic means and whether or not transiently or incidentally to some other use of this publication) without the permission of the copyright owner.

British Library Cataloguing-in-Publication Data
A catalogue record for this book is available from the British Library

ISBN paperback: 978-1-906733-84-1
ISBN ebook: 978-1-906733-88-9

CONTENTS

Contents

INTRODUCTION

1999: the final year of the millennium and, to be more precise, the end of the first real century of cinema. At just over 100 years young, cinema had grown from simple unedited one shot wonders such as *Train Arriving at a Station* (1895) to bloated blockbuster behemoths of over three hours in length. Cinema was very much about spectacle at the end of the century and audiences lapped up explosive, visual effects laden blockbusters in their millions.

Cinema in the 20th century became a huge business with multinational conglomerates competing for global audiences by offering international stars, the latest special effects and corporate synergy that meant films were just one part in a bigger branding strategy that would continue to fill a studio's pockets long after a film was released and then removed from cinemas.

1999 should have been the year of *Star Wars*. After a 16 year wait, fans of George Lucas' blockbuster science fiction franchise were eagerly expecting the return to a galaxy far, far away that was promised with the release of *Star Wars Episode I: The Phantom Menace* (1999). Fans of the *Star Wars* saga since childhood had sky high expectations for Lucas' prequel that would see the back story of how young Anakin Skywalker became the dastardly Darth Vader. All grown up now, many of these fans were in for quite a shock and a crash landing back to Earth, for which Lucas would never quite be forgiven.

Despite some disappointment, *Star Wars Episode I* did however go on to become the biggest winner at the box office in 1999. With a $115 million budget, it eventually made over a billion dollars across the globe, making it both a huge success and incredibly profitable for 20th Century Fox.

However 1999 was also a pivotal moment in the future of film production and it was another very different film that made an equally, if not far more, significant splash at the box office. *The Blair Witch Project* (1999) was a tiny budget independent horror film that unlike *Star Wars*, no one had ever heard of at the beginning of the year. There was no in-built fan base, no special effects, no stars or promise of anything approaching the imaginative planets and alien creatures of *Star Wars*. Made for a tiny fraction of the *The Phantom Menace's* budget, *The Blair Witch Project* may not have made over a billion dollars at the box office but it became easily the most profitable film of the year and one of the most profitable films of all time. Fighting its way to nearly $250 million worldwide, *The Blair Witch Project* made back nearly 10,000 times its production budget at the box office compared to the *Star Wars* prequel making roughly ten times its own budget back.

To put this into even sharper perspective, *The Blair Witch Project* with its tiny budget and horror genre trappings was the tenth biggest box office earner of 1999, nearly beating the romantic-comedy reunion (after the hugely successful *Pretty Woman* (1990)) of Julia Roberts and Richard Gere in *Runaway Bride*. Not only that, *The Blair Witch Project* did beat Tom Hanks in *The Green Mile*, nineteenth Bond film *The World is Not Enough*, Richard Curtis rom-com *Notting Hill* and Will Smith's blockbuster mess *Wild, Wild West*.

Even with strong competition in the horror genre, *The Blair Witch Project* managed to stand out from the rest. *The Sixth Sense* starring Bruce Willis and the biggest twist of the year got people talking and managed to become the second biggest film of the year behind *Star Wars*. Universal's *The Mummy* remake on the other hand only managed to sneak in to the box office chart two places above *The Blair Witch Project*. Far bigger budget horror efforts such as *Sleepy Hollow*, *The Haunting* and *End of Days* could not come close to *The Blair Witch Project's* box office draw even with the likes of Johnny Depp, Arnold Schwarzenegger and the promise of bucket loads of CGI crammed into the trailers.

The big budget action adventure and CGI filled template for modern horror may have led to some success for *The Mummy* but it appeared audiences might already be tiring of seeing digitally rendered pixels up on screen and were beginning to search for something simpler. Despite *Star Wars'* inevitable success, other big films of 1999 included the subversive likes of *American Beauty* and *Fight Club*, and even the spectacular visual feast of *The Matrix* had some intellectual undertones in amongst the action.

Horror fans, however, had been feeling a little concerned over the direction that the genre had been taking over the past decade. The blockbuster budgets of the likes of *The Haunting* might be able to provide fancy computer generated horrors but where were the actual scares? Released in 1996, Wes Craven's *Scream* (1996) had revitalised the slasher sub-genre, bringing in lashings of irony, self-referential humour and knowing winks to the horror fans in the audience. The sequel did much of the same a year later with countless imitators such as *I Know What You Did Last Summer* (1997) and *Urban Legend* (1998) crowding the multiplexes but offering little of the wit and smarts of *Scream*. Horror seemed trapped in a renewed slasher cycle with interchangeably sexy teens being offed by another round of masked killers, none as menacing or memorable as the icons of the 1980s. Horror needed something fresh; a back to basics approach that could really deliver the thrills that horror fans desired.

Horror has always been a genre that has skirted the mainstream. Tapping into audiences' fears and anxieties, horror films have never been products that can be sold to a mass audience. Some people will avoid horror at all costs; others will seek out horror above anything else. Fans of the horror genre are often notoriously devoted to their favourite films but also to the genre as a whole and what it has to offer. However, on some occasions, horror films have also managed to break into the public consciousness in a far bigger and more profound way. Look at the impact of honorary horror films *Jaws* (1975) or *Alien* (1979) for example. Some films tap into the zeitgeist, pulling in mainstream audiences and exceeding all expectations of box office figures normally produced by films in this often overlooked genre. However, it is never certain which films will break out of the horror ghetto and start to ensnare wider audiences in their grip.

As a result of this generally niche audience and cautious predictions over what horror films can achieve in cinemas, budgets for horror films are mostly kept low. From the British Hammer Studios films to Roger Corman's adaptations of Edgar Allen Poe's short stories, horror films have made do with limited budgets in order to be able to turn a quick profit. When horror hit the screens of the 1970s, a new wave of vicious, frequently very violent and exploitative pictures were released under the direction of the likes of Wes Craven, George A. Romero and John Carpenter. These low budget horror classics such as *Night of the Living Dead* (1968), *Last House on the Left* (1972), *The Texas Chain Saw Massacre* (1974) and *Halloween* (1978) brought the horrors of the Vietnam War home to an increasingly troubled and unstable America. Often banned as much for their visceral effect as for the amount of gore they actually showed, these films were made for very little money but had huge impacts on audiences and still remain culturally relevant and significant to academic scholars and horror fans today.

The 1980s saw many *Halloween* imitators emerge and with the slasher cycle spewing out endless sequels to films starring Freddy Krueger and Jason Vorhees, the special effects of gory make up and prosthetics made the 'less is more' mantra of earlier horror films redundant. When *Scream* came along and revitalised the slasher sub-genre at the end of the 1990s, it seemed the irony and splatter of modern horror was slipping into repetition, formula and self-parody. Enter *The Blair Witch Project*.

The Blair Witch Project was arguably a product of its time more than any other film of the 1990s. It signalled the approaching end of an era and spectacularly heralded the advent of digital filmmaking. The studios were focussed more than ever on big blockbusters like James Cameron's $200 million *Titanic* (1997) but independent films were finding new means of production, distribution and even exhibition that would change the industry forever. First editors switched from analogue to digital methods of cutting films, then the soundtracks swiftly went digital, starting with *Dick Tracy* (1990). Animation took leaps and bounds forward in the 1990s. James Cameron's *Terminator 2: Judgment Day* (1991) introduced incredible morphing effects, *Toy Story* (1995) became the first film fully made within a computer and *Jurassic Park* (1993), *Titanic* and *Gladiator* (2000) all furthered the technology and made the impossible now possible on film.

Most importantly for low budget filmmakers, new and improved lightweight digital video cameras were being introduced. Incredibly cheap to shoot with compared to traditional celluloid, these cameras revolutionised independent filmmaking and opened it up to a vastly increased number of potential participants in low budget production. Woody Allen, Mathieu Kassovitz and Lars von Trier proved directors could make critically lauded work on inexpensive cameras with handheld cinematography that many considered the aesthetics of increased gritty realism. It was *The Blair Witch Project* that took this to a new level and defined the era.

With its camcorder and 16mm filmed footage, its aesthetic became its unique selling point and its *raison d'être*. The gritty visuals, total lack of CG effects or even grisly prosthetics and make up, made *The Blair Witch Project* the saving grace that horror fans had been waiting for. Backed up by an internet marketing campaign, *The Blair Witch Project* became a glowing example of what could be achieved with cheap emerging technology, imagination and a less is more approach. By the year 2000 and due to the influx of digital video cameras, there were far more independent features being made than ever before.

This book will explore the aesthetics of *The Blair Witch Project*, how identification is encouraged in the film and the way it successfully creates fear in contemporary audiences. The final chapter will explore the marketing, reception and legacy of *The Blair Witch Project*.

PLOT OUTLINE

White text on a plain black background states: 'In October of 1994 three student filmmakers disappeared in the woods near Burkittsville, Maryland while shooting a documentary. A year later their footage was found.'

Director Heather, soundman Mike and cameraman Josh are embarking on making a student documentary project on the mysterious events that surround the local legend of the Blair Witch. After interviewing some locals and stocking up on supplies, the trio head into the woods. They film at locations that are notorious for their roles in the events of the Blair Witch legend and while filming for the documentary, Heather also films behind the scenes footage. The first night in the woods, Josh claims to have heard noises like cackling in the night. The following night they hear noises all around them like cracking wood. The next morning Josh argues the noises were probably made by locals trying to scare them. They become lost while hiking out of the woods and tensions rise as Heather continues to film everything including their arguments.

Every night that they camp in the woods, stranger things happen. They have lost their map, begin running low on food and become increasingly desperate to get out of the woods. One night Josh disappears from the tent and Heather and Mike resort to slowly continuing to walk during the day before setting up camp again at dark. The following night, Heather directly addresses the camera and apologises to Mike and Josh and their families. She takes responsibility for what is happening, understanding now that they are being hunted by something. She apologises to her parents and breaks down, hyperventilating and terrified. They hear Josh calling for help and follow the sound. Discovering a derelict house, Mike and Heather rush in. On entering the basement there is a bump and Mike's camera falls to the ground. Heather then sees Mike standing in the corner facing the wall, before there is another bump and her camera also drops to the floor. Heather's screaming stops but the camera keeps rolling for a few seconds before the credits begin.

CHRONOLOGY OF THE BLAIR WITCH MYTHOLOGY

February, 1785: Several children accuse Elly Kedward of luring them into her home to draw blood from them. Kedward is found guilty of witchcraft, banished from the village during a particularly harsh winter and presumed dead.

November, 1786: By midwinter all of Kedward's accusers along with half of the town's children vanish. Fearing a curse, the townspeople flee Blair and vow never to utter Elly Kedward's name again.

November, 1809: The Blair Witch Cult is published. This rare book, commonly considered fiction, tells of an entire town cursed by an outcast witch.

1824: Burkittsville is founded on the Blair site.

August, 1825: Eleven witnesses testify to seeing a pale woman's hand reach up and pull ten-year-old Eileen Treacle into Tappy East Creek. Her body is never recovered, and for thirteen days after the drowning the creek is clogged with oily bundles of sticks.

March, 1886: Eight-year-old Robin Weaver is reported missing and search parties are dispatched. Although Weaver returns, one of the search parties does not. Their bodies are found weeks later at Coffin Rock tied together and disemboweled.

November, 1940 – May, 1941: Starting with Emily Hollands, a total of seven children are abducted from the area surrounding Burkittsville, Maryland.

May 25, 1941: An old hermit named Rustin Parr walks into a local market and tells the people there that he is 'finally finished'. After police hike for four hours to his secluded house in the woods, they find the bodies of seven missing children in the cellar. Each child has been ritualistically murdered and disembowelled. Parr admits to everything in detail, telling authorities that he did it for 'an old woman ghost' who occupied the woods near his house. He is quickly convicted and hanged.

October 20, 1994: Montgomery College students Heather Donahue, Joshua Leonard and Michael Williams arrive in Burkittsville to interview locals about the legend of the Blair Witch for a class project. Heather interviews Mary Brown, an old and quite insane woman who has lived in the area all her life. Mary claims to have seen the Blair Witch one day near Tappy Creek in the form of a hairy, half-human, half-animal beast.

October 21, 1994: In the early morning Heather interviews two fishermen who tell the filmmakers that Coffin Rock is less than twenty minutes from town and easily accessible by an old logging trail. The filmmakers hike into Black Hills Forest shortly thereafter and are never seen again.

October 25, 1994: The first APB is issued. Josh's car is found later in the day parked on Black Rock Road.

October 26, 1994: The Maryland State Police launch their search of the Black Hills area, an operation that lasts ten days and includes up to one hundred men aided by dogs, helicopters, and even a fly over by a Department of Defense Satellite.

November 5, 1994: The search is called off after 33,000 man hours fail to find a trace of the filmmakers or any of their gear. Heather's mother, Angie Donahue, begins an exhaustive personal search for her daughter and her two companions.

June 19, 1995: The case is declared inactive and unsolved.

October 16, 1995: Students from the University of Maryland's Anthropology Department discover a duffel bag containing film cans, DAT tapes, video-cassettes, a Hi-8 video camera, Heather's journal and a CP-16 film camera buried under the foundation of a 100 year-old cabin. When the evidence is examined, Burkittsville Sheriff Ron Cravens announced that the 11 rolls of black and white film and 10 HI8 video tapes are indeed the property of Heather Donahue and her crew.

December 15, 1995: After an initial study of the bag's contents, select pieces of film footage are shown to the families. According to Angie Donahue, there are several unusual events but nothing conclusive. The families question the thoroughness of the analysis and demanded another look.

February 19, 1996: The families are shown a second group of clips that local law enforcement officials consider to be faked. Outraged, Mrs. Donahue goes public with her criticism and Sheriff Cravens restricts all access to the evidence; a restriction that two lawsuits fail to lift.

March 1, 1996: The Sheriff's department announces that the evidence is inconclusive and the case is once again declared inactive and unsolved. The footage is to be released to the families when the legal limit of its classification runs out, on October 16, 1997.

October 16, 1997: The found footage of their children's last days is turned over to the families of Heather Donahue, Joshua Leonard, and Michael Williams. Angie Donahue contracts Haxan Films to examine the footage and piece together the events of October 20 – 28, 1994.

REFERENCES

http://www.blairwitch.com/mythology.html

1. THE MAKING OF THE BLAIR WITCH PROJECT

The stories that surround the production of *The Blair Witch Project* are as fascinating as the final product. The circumstances of the film's low-budget production are legendary with stories of the cast being filled with real fear by the 'method' directing techniques of the two directors. From developing the script and financing the film to the extensive post-production period and taking the finished product to the Sundance Film Festival, the entire process is an inspiring example of inventive independent filmmaking.

The Blair Witch Project is a film that could not have been made without advancements in camera technology beyond the early days of cinema. In the past, the cameras used to make films were large, loud and highly immobile. They also required expensive film stock that made film production a very costly process. Smaller cameras that shoot on video and therefore cost far less to produce the footage are absolutely essential for filming out in the woods for days and days on end. Also, there is the increased intimacy that these cameras allow and the fact that they can be operated by non-professionals. Like Neo-realist, New Wave and vérité filmmakers that took lighter weight cameras into the streets, directors Daniel Myrick and Eduardo Sánchez used modern video cameras that are highly mobile and easily manoeuvred. They invite intimacy, as seen in the confessional moments of the film where the camera is positioned in Heather's face as she cries and apologises to her family.

Modern, cheap cameras that are small and easy to hold and move do tend to produce a lower quality of image. However they can also tell the viewer more about the person holding the camera. These small handheld devices register the movement of the operator which increases the identification a viewer feels with the camera operator. The lack of tripod usage means that the viewer gets a better sense of the movement and therefore potentially the state-of-mind of the operator. Camcorders can record the emotions of the user by making audiences speculate about the person who is holding (and shaking) the camera. This is another key to understanding the pleasures of *The Blair Witch Project* for horror fans that wish to be terrified. Not only is what is on screen often terrifying, but the hand that records it is also terrified. It is frantic and out of control, giving the viewer even more reason to be afraid. It is a more visceral experience if the character that controls the camera is lacking in control. Not allowing the viewer to see what is happening to the camera operator can also instill fear. If a character pans the camera quickly left to right, the viewer might wonder what has caused their swift movement. Therefore these modern, small and easily manoeuvrable cameras were absolutely essential to the directors of *The Blair Witch Project*.

INFLUENCES

Going all the way back to 18th century literature, Harris (2001: 75-76) has noted the influence of epistolary novels on *The Blair Witch Project*. An epistolary novel is one that is written as a series of documents, most commonly letters written by either a single or multiple protagonists. Therefore the reader of such novels only hears the story from one point of view, the main character that 'writes' the letter or diary entry. In *The Blair Witch Project*, we witness the video 'diary' of the protagonists.

There have been numerous attempts in the past to offer a faked representation of reality by creating media products that, while not genuine, appear to tell the 'truth'. Higley and Weinstock (2004: 13-14) point to the 'ghost photographs so popular at the turn of the 20th century' that suggest to an observer that something extraordinary has occurred and been captured by a keen camera operator. Many would consider the photographs as proof of the existence of ghosts whereas many others would seek to find out the 'truth' behind what is depicted in the photographs. Similarly, audiences of *The Blair Witch Project* find a conflict over the veracity of how it is filmed and the (perhaps) fantastical occurrences that are represented. Its appearance as a documentary led to countless debates over its truthfulness with many early viewers of the film fooled by its ploy.

The Blair Witch Project, like the radio production of H. G. Wells's *The War of the Worlds* (1938), 'depicts a fantastic situation as though it were fact' (Higley and Weinstock, 2004: 14). The stories of Orson Welles's radio production suggest that his faked news report was so convincing that some listeners genuinely feared that Earth was being attacked by aliens. Countless sources attest to the fact that many adult listeners reportedly required medical treatment for shock and hysteria. The hoax worked because the broadcast authentically simulated how radio worked in an emergency. This authentic simulation in *The Blair Witch Project* was created by the publicity (including a website and 'missing' posters) and the film's style that also helped to convince some early viewers that they were watching the real footage of a group of film students who disappeared in extraordinary circumstances in the woods. There are many stories reported of people travelling to the town of Burkittsville where the events of the film take place in order to search for the students. Since then, fans of the film have repeatedly stolen the Burkittsville 'welcome' sign.

An infamous film that came before *The Blair Witch Project* and used similar techniques, such as mock-documentary footage and pretending the cast were deceased, was Ruggero Deodato's *Cannibal Holocaust* (1980). While this film never claims to be entirely made up of the recording of documentary filmmakers, a significant portion of the film is taken up with footage supposedly recorded by a trio of filmmakers who disappeared in the Amazonian jungle. This film is notorious for blurring the lines between fact and fiction, with the real murder of animals used in the film and gory special effects that are still scarily plausible to this day. This early example of found footage undoubtedly had an influence on Myrick and Sánchez when making their own film.

A controversial predecessor of *The Blair Witch Project* is a film that was released only a year before to much lesser fanfare. *The Last Broadcast* (1998), made by a different pair of young filmmakers, Stefan Avalos and Lance Weiler, has many clear similarities with *The Blair Witch Project* that have led to a lot of accusations that Myrick and Sánchez plagiarised it. In an article for Fangoria, Sarah Kendzior (1999: 36) argues the case of *The Last Broadcast* and its filmmakers suggesting that there are similarities 'not only to plot and structure but to their respective websites, promotional tactics and even title logos'. She also claims there has been a 'reluctance of those involved with *Blair Witch* to comment on the earlier project' and suggests that this should arouse suspicion. *The Last Broadcast* is another mock-documentary that features filmmakers getting lost and disappearing in the woods while shooting a reality TV show investigating local legend the 'Jersey Devil'. So far, so *Blair Witch*, but where the films really differ is in their presentation of the lost filmmakers' footage, a point that will be returned to later in this chapter.

WRITING

The Blair Witch Project started as an idea, referred to by the directing duo as far back as 1993 as *The Woods Movie*. The directors Eduardo Sánchez and Daniel Myrick took the seed of this idea and wrote a script that was only 35 pages long. When doubts over the originality of the idea were put forward by those aware of its predecessor *The Last Broadcast*, Haxan Films suggested that the idea was registered with the Writers' Guild of America in 1996, with Sánchez saying the concept for the film was originated in 1992. Though there might be some discrepancies over the exact year the idea was conceived, it appears to have been long before *The Last Broadcast* was made or released.

This early incarnation of the idea was really less of a script and more of a detailed treatment or outline of the film's narrative. There was no scripted dialogue, a decision the directors deliberately made to encourage as much improvisation from the cast as possible. Sánchez says in an interview with the A.V. Club (1999) that they 'didn't want to put those kinds of limitations on the actors'. Having no dialogue forces the cast to make up their lines on the spot. Their characters become free flowing constructions. Though this can cause the need for far more editing in the post-production stages with vast amounts of unusable footage, it can also create moments of realistic spontaneity in keeping with the film's mockumentary and vérité style aesthetics.

The Blair Witch Project was originally conceived of as a more traditional mock-documentary with the footage shot by the actors only meant to feature in the last part of the documentary on the curse of the Blair Witch through the ages. It was only after the footage Heather and Mike filmed was returned to the directors and editing had begun that the idea to use only this footage in the feature was initiated. In essence, the writing of the film was limited on the page and to a greater extent it wrote itself in the improvisation of the production and the editing in the post-production stage.

FUNDING

Even a film as cheap and as aesthetically 'basic' as *The Blair Witch Project* requires some financial backing to allow for its extremely modest production budget. The cost of making a film like this would be extremely small compared to the big Hollywood studio machine that churns out special effects-driven blockbusters that are now creeping up to $300 million per film.

The Blair Witch Project was just one of many in a long line of independently financed films that made huge profits from tiny budgets. The tales of how some of these films have been financed are now legendary. Robert Rodriguez sold the use of his body for medical experiments to fund his debut *El Mariachi* (1992), made for a measly $7,000. Kevin Smith maxed out as many credit cards as he could to raise the $27,000 needed to shoot his debut *Clerks* (1994). Horror has a long history of independent low budget movie production with John Carpenter's *Halloween* being made for $320,000 and another seminal slasher *Friday the 13th* (1980) being made for $650,000.

According to Sánchez, 'the original budget to get the film in the can was probably between $20,000 and $25,000. Then, once we got to Sundance to make a print and do a sound mix, we were probably more in the neighbourhood of $100,000' (Young, 2009). The early stages of the film cost next to nothing with the filmmakers being so thrifty with their available funds that they even bought one of the cameras then shot the film and returned it in time to get a full refund.

However, before shooting could commence, the filmmakers still had to raise the money needed for the initial budget. In order to do this, they created an eight minute trailer for the film in order to get investors interested. This mini-documentary was all about the disappearance of three student filmmakers in the woods while making their documentary about the Blair Witch. Myrick and Sánchez would play the short film as real, convincing audiences of its veracity through the use of fake newspaper articles and news footage. It provided an overview of the back-story and developing mythology and said that Haxan films intended to acquire this sensational and unbelievable 'real' footage.

Without shooting any of the actual film yet, the directors managed to gain the interest of John Pierson, an independent film enthusiast who had been quietly supporting small films for years. Pierson had collected film business contacts when he was a programmer at influential art theatres in New York City. When young directors started asking him to help them get their films sold, he began contributing financial support and taking films to distributors and studios in order to get them distribution deals. Pierson later started a half hour television show called *Spilt Screen* (1997-2001) in which he would drive around America in search of interesting independent filmmakers.

When Pierson saw the eight minute teaser of *The Blair Witch Project* that Myrick and Sánchez had made, he was completely taken in by its convincing representation of the fake events. Pierson said 'I can't believe all of this. I've never heard about it' to which Myrick replied, 'John, we made it all up.' Pierson ran a segment on *Split Screen* about *The Blair Witch Project* and played the footage without revealing to the audience that it was fake. It appears that he was not the only one fooled. The reactions on Pierson's bulletin board told a similar story. People believed that what they had just seen was real. An Albany detective even called in to offer his help in finding the 'lost' filmmakers. People posting on the bulletin board soon started discussing the morality of the faked footage after Pierson came clean.

While the filmmakers decided that they did not want to explicitly state that the film was a real piece of evidence of a disappearance, the short film had the desired effect in generating interest in the project. Grainy Pictures, Pierson's company, decided to invest $10,000 in the film. Everyone who saw the footage was intrigued and before being told that it was a hoax, would ask if the filmmakers had access to the tapes with the rest of the footage on them.

However the budget of *The Blair Witch Project* did not remain quite as legendarily low as it first appeared. As Sánchez already said, more money was spent once the film got into the Sundance Film Festival and then when it was bought by Artisan Entertainment, they spent another half a million dollars on it. According to Sánchez, 'they did a new sound mix, and they had us re-shoot some stuff. They didn't like the original ending with Mike standing in the corner. They asked us to shoot some new endings — Mike hanging by his neck; Mike crucified on a big stick figure; Mike with his shirt ripped open and all bloodied. We shot them but ended up staying with our original ending. So the budget of what you saw in the theatres was probably $500,000 to $750,000' (Young, 2009).

It is interesting to note the pressure that the distributors put the filmmakers under to shoot a slightly more conventional and 'satisfying' ending. This process is common in studio filmmaking with test screenings often leading to changes that will supposedly make the film more commercially successful by appealing to a wider audience. If the producers of David Fincher's *Seven* (1995) had had their way, for example (spoiler alert!), there is no way that the film would have ended with the severed head of the hero's wife in a box. What is even more interesting is that despite this, Artisan chose to keep the original ending and have faith in the unique and disturbing quality of the filmmakers' original intentions. *The Blair Witch Project* has been praised for its abrupt ending and the shock of its final frames. The ambiguity and untidiness of it all are critical parts of what made it such a powerful and realistic experience.

CASTING

The casting of the three leads was absolutely essential to the success of *The Blair Witch Project*. Heather, Mike and Josh needed to be completely believable as amateur film students and even more importantly they had to be unrecognisable actors who could handle the demands of constant improvisation and a fully immersive shoot, out in the woods over the course of several days.

Daniel Myrick said in an interview with *The House of Horrors* (1999) that they auditioned over 2000 actors over the course of a year in order to find the right actors and cast the roles. The directors were looking for impeccable improvisational skills as well as the right personalities for the characters.

Advertisements were placed in the publication Backstage which is aimed at those working in the entertainment industry and specifically for helping with casting. The advertisements highlighted that the feature film would be heavily improvised, shot in a wooded location and seemed to be deterring people from applying for the roles. Heather Donahue was initially put off when she arrived at the auditions and there were further signs indicating that if the actors had already tried improvisation, then they too would probably not be suitable. It became very clear that the directors wanted completely natural actors, untainted by years of experience and unafraid of not being pampered on a typical film set.

On making it past the deterrents, those continuing into the actual audition found themselves thrown into an off-the-cuff improvisation, according to actor Joshua Leonard (Mannes, 1999). The directors would immediately say 'You've been in jail for the last nine years. We're the parole board. Why should we let you go?' Those that could not spring into character in an instant were shown the door. Actors used to more traditional auditions where they are asked to deliver a monologue, act in a scene or simply read from a script would not make it through to the next round of auditions.

Not only did Myrick and Sánchez want to be sure their chosen cast had the necessary improvisational skills, but they also had to be sure that the actors would be tough enough to handle the physical and emotional demands of what would become a legendary and unique shoot. No catering, no makeup, no costumes and no script. These guys were on their own.

FILMING

It was originally conceived that the film would be shot entirely on black-and-white 16mm film as the filmmakers thought it made things look more terrifying than video. However, producer Gregg Hale suggested that due to the relative cheapness of shooting on video, some of the footage should be captured with a more modest film stock. Eventually the directors decided that it would not be unreasonable for Heather to have her own Hi-8 camera with her for filming behind the scenes footage and this would allow more to be shot with cheaper stock. It also made for an interesting contrast between the film and video footage and the more haphazard and informal footage of what occurred behind the scenes.

The actual filming of The Blair Witch Project took eight days, a tight shooting schedule even by ordinary independent film standards. It began in October 1997, months after that other horror mock-doc The Last Broadcast had already started to gain some positive attention even though it had not yet been screened in theatres or at festivals. Though Myrick and Sánchez had not yet seen The Last Broadcast, some would claim that they had already been influenced by the similar sounding horror film.

Heather, Michael and Joshua spent seven days capturing almost every second of footage that is in the finished film. After being given two days of training on the film equipment that they would be using throughout the shoot, production began. A sound expert trained Michael on using the DAT and getting levels right and Myrick took Joshua out to get him familiar with using the 16mm film camera.

Unlike traditionally shot horror films, the actors would shoot the film themselves. Even later found footage films since *The Blair Witch Project* have not demonstrated this commitment to realism, instead opting to still employ professional directors of photography and camera operators to shoot the majority of their footage. *The Blair Witch Project* took realism as its prime directive and completely disregarded the conventions of making a fiction feature film, even a low budget independent one. Its progeny, which include the likes of *Paranormal Activity* (2007), *[REC]* (2007) and *Cloverfield* (2008), did not dare go as far as to have the majority of the footage shot by the cast. It was an extremely experimental and risky way of shooting a feature film.

Furthermore, the directors would not even be present in the woods with the actors. Myrick and Sánchez stayed well away once filming started and left the actors to capture the footage and explore their characters in their own ways. By distancing cast and crew, the actors would be free from time consuming set ups and the distractions of modern film making. They were free to shoot and left to fend for themselves in the unfamiliar woods. Props were only what they took with them and the locations were all natural. The directors only interfered with the 'sets' before the cast approached and were virtually unseen by Heather, Michael and Joshua throughout the eight days of shooting in the town and woods.

The actors were required to use their own names so Heather Donohue, Michael C. Williams and Joshua Leonard became the Heather, Mike and Josh of the finished feature. This technique meant that they would be less likely to break character and even if they did, the footage might still be salvaged when the directors came to edit it. During filming, if they became hungry, fed up and began getting agitated with each other, as long as the camera remained on, the footage could potentially be used. Tensions, arguments and even screaming matches all became fair game if the actors were all using their real names. This tension between the characters and the urge in particular of Heather to keep filming also helped define Heather's character and made Donahue's job as an actress easier. She acknowledged in an interview for Starburst Magazine (1999: 55) that 'a considerable part of my character came out of the fact that somehow I had to justify keeping a camera in people's faces in times of extreme distress... That was really a starting point for me, because it's a specific kind of person who could do that.'

With no script to work from, no camera directions and not even any character names to remember, the cast were almost completely free from outside interference and left to improvise their own reality in the woods. However, directors Myrick and Sánchez still had a story to tell and therefore the actors still had marks to meet, beats to hit and a destination to reach. Despite relinquishing a certain amount of control, the directors still asserted their will and 'directed' the shoot from afar. Though they were unseen by the cast, the directors would interact with their actors through a number of other means.

The need for actors able to improvise effectively would be essential as the directors would not be there with directions. No matter what was thrown at them, the actors' reactions had to appear genuine and 'in character'. Instead of having the directors with the actors on location, Myrick and Sánchez would leave mysterious bundles, rock piles and stick figures around for the cast to discover. They would slime the backpacks of the characters and make frightening noises in the night, at one point even attacking their tent to scare the cast. The real confusion, anxiety and terror that the cast may have felt is easy to imagine but without immediate improvisational skills, the footage and the performances would have lacked realism and the necessary urgency created by the directors' actions.

Myrick, Sánchez and the small team from their Haxan production company attempted to create the perfect conditions for improvising. At the same time, they wanted the cast to have to imagine as little as possible what their characters would be feeling in any given scenario. The cast would look around and see no crew members and the only cameras were being carried by their fellow cast members. Myrick and Sánchez dubbed their approach 'method filmmaking' after the family of techniques used by actors (from Marlon Brando to Christian Bale) known as 'The Method'. Definitions of method acting differ but the fundamental point is that a method actor will go to great lengths to immerse themselves in the character they are playing. *The Blair Witch Project* directors forced their actors into immersion by leaving them in the woods and restricting their contact with the world outside the diegetic world of the film narrative.

This approach was also based on producer Gregg Hale's military training. Hale had been through Survival, Evasion, Resistance and Escape (SERE) training whilst in the army that involved four days of being chased by American soldiers pretending to hunt for him.

He spoke of his terror despite knowing that soon the ordeal would be over and that the soldiers were simply playing a part. The idea was to put the cast of *The Blair Witch Project* through a similarly immersive experience, physically and mentally abusing them or breaking them down so that their performances would not require much imagination or perhaps what could be called 'real' acting. Sánchez spoke of building a 'tunnel of reality around them' (Pincus, 1999) by keeping them in a manufactured reality where they could never be sure what was real and what was fake. By the end of the shoot, the hunger, the cold, the exhaustion, the confusion and the terror felt by the actors would be stimuli that they could use in their performances. Hale said in an interview with Starburst Magazine that 'normally your conscious mind insulates you from extreme fear. But if we could wear down the actors mentally and physically, by the end of the film when really intense things are happening they'd tap into a part of the psyche they normally don't touch. The insulation would be stripped off and they'd react in a more primal way' (1999: 58).

Starting on day one of the shoot when Heather, Mike and Josh are interviewing the local townspeople about the legend of the Blair Witch, the cast were instructed only very briefly by the directors about where to go and who to interview. As a result, Heather, Mike and Josh interviewed a mixture of planted actors and genuine people on the streets of the town. Both the acting extras and real people end up in the final film, some having heard of the Blair Witch mythology and some not. Despite the complete fabrication of the mythology by the filmmakers, there are people interviewed on camera that were not planted extras that claim to have heard of the witch, such as the woman on the street with her small child in her arms.

The planted extras served an extra function, as they would be tasked with giving the central trio clues and directions of where to go next and who to interview if they wanted to find out more. Joshua Leonard said in an interview: 'We'd start interviewing people and the plants that they had in there would say, "Oh, you gotta go check out old Miss Mary Brown who lives down in the trailer shed." So then we'd go interview Mary Brown. And we had seeds, we had seeds to work from, that's what they gave us was always … just enough to initiate a conversation and then the rest of it was completely on our backs to improv and roll with the situation at hand' (Mannes, 1999).

This woman was not a plant, yet still claimed to have heard stories of something scary in the woods.

However, it is only once Heather, Mike and Joshua get to the woods that the torment, confusion, isolation and mind games really began. The film makers wanted as little contact with the cast as possible. They kept track of them through the use of Global Positioning Satellite technology and kept them away from roads and other signs of civilisation as they were left almost to their own devices in the Seneca Creek State Park in Maryland. The GPS allowed the small crew to track the progress of the cast within the 6,300 acres of the park and ensure their safety. The cast were also given a CB radio and had a code word between them which they could use whenever they needed to break the scenario. The CB radio was not supposed to be used unless there was real danger but the GPS unit meant that the filmmakers could leave their limited directions for the cast at certain pre-programmed locations.

According to the stars of the film, they were guided to milk crates each day that contained three plastic canisters. By using their GPS units, the three would end up at their wait points and in each of the three canisters they found would be a note, one for each actor/character. The secrecy, distrust and tension created between the characters would no doubt stem in some small part from the lack of knowledge each actor had about what the other cast members' note said. The Haxan production team would leave the notes to guide what the character would be thinking, feeling and doing, but only vaguely, and therefore still leaving the dialogue to total improvisation. The actors were free to create the scenes and take their characters as far as they wanted, bearing in mind the directorial notes.

Heather Donahue spoke of the process, revealing in an interview that 'you always knew something big was coming when your note would read something like: "When you pass the big log with a sign, make sure the camera is on." We'd all look at each other and we're like, OK, you guys ready? This is gonna be a big one. Then you're like, all right, I'm feeling the fear. Then we'd go check it out, and we'd shoot it' (McEnery, 1999). She also commented on the note she received from the directors before her famous confession scene. It said that she was going to die and had to make amends to all the people she had hurt and that she should attempt to die with as clear a conscience as possible. All her words were improvised and her complete despair is palpable. The iconic framing of the shot that only reveals the top half of her face was also a happy accident as Donahue had thought she was composing a complete shot of her face.

While the suggestion that the cast steeled themselves for the big moments hints that the trio were not completely immersed in their characters 24 hours a day and did have breaks from not only shooting, but being in character, they still spent seven days straight in the woods with only one brief period of respite. The directors had programmed 'escape routes' into the GPS systems and after 24 hours of rain, the cast decided to use one. They ended up at a house where Donahue reveals they were invited in for hot cocoa and got to use a real toilet (Lim, 1999).

Apart from this, the cast really did endure the shoot without the traditional comforts associated with even the most basic of film sets. There was no craft services, no toilets, no chances to see their performances played back to them on a monitor and no feedback from their directors on how they were doing. They had to carry 60 pound packs on their backs and the directors kept them moving increasing distances on each day and with dwindling sources of supplies. Along with their notes, the cast would find small rations of food in the mystery milk crates. However these supplies were deliberately lessened each day to make the cast hungrier, more agitated and more exhausted. By the last two days of the shoot, Heather and Michael, the two remaining cast members, were only being fed a single Power Bar and a banana per day. If the characters were hungry, so should the actors be. 'By applying the same physical and mental stresses to the actors— lack of food, lack of sleep, walking them around, fucking with them at night,' says Hale, 'we hoped by the time we really needed them to freak out, they would be able to tap into areas of their psyche they normally wouldn't be able to tap into' (Kaufman, 1999).

The crew had to keep ahead of their cast; camping close by but out of sight, leaving them their notes and supplies and terrifying them during the cold, dark nights. They would terrorise the campers; making noises and playing sounds through boomboxes and then leaving creepy objects around for them to find in the mornings. The cast would have little idea of what to expect and therefore their surprise in the film feels real. The cast are almost as freaked out as the characters would be. When Heather exclaims 'what the fuck was that?' during one of the nights, she is reacting to a crew member dressed all in white and running alongside her, a sight that the camera (un)fortunately could not pick up.

The majority of the film was shot in one take, with the actors capturing their footage as it happened and without rehearsal or reshoots. The only scenes that were not filmed in the first takes are the moment Heather and Mike discover the package containing a tooth and some blood and the final shot of Mike facing the corner. Originally Heather threw away the package without getting a good look inside it and the crew decided to step in and get her to film it again, ensuring the audience would see what was in there. The final scene, as discussed earlier, was reshot under the direction of Artisan when they bought the film but they still decided to go with the original ending. However when this was first filmed by Heather, the shot of Mike in the corner was not clear and required a reshoot. By the time they got to filming the final scene the actors were clearly feeling the pressure and their nerves were fried. "The house was genuinely scary for me because we didn't know what we'd be coming across," insists Williams in an interview with Starburst Magazine:

> My notes said, 'When you hear something tonight, follow it. When you find out where it brings you to, go all the way up'. I'm like 'What the heck is this?' I actually had to radio Ed because I didn't know what we were going to get into and I figured, 'This has gotta be the last thing and I don't want to screw it up.' I radioed Ed and said, 'Ed you

Mike faces the corner in one of the film's chilling final frames.

gotta come and talk to me.' So he actually came and said, 'You'll understand when you see what is going on'. He wouldn't tell me. (1999: 57)

The limiting of directors' control over the actors is a daring and unpredictable ploy that could have gone wrong in many ways. Leaving so much of the production process in the hands of the actors might bring many benefits but there were also potentially huge risks. The directors reveal that they spent a lot of time watching from afar and worrying about what the cast were doing. They had concerns with the safety of the cast, the crew and the equipment. One crew member fell in the creek late one night while scaring the cast and the other crew members had to share their dry clothes to avoid hypothermia while hiking him out of the woods. While the cast crossed the log bridge in one scene, the crew were incredibly worried that if they slipped and fell, the equipment would be ruined. One of the cameras did in fact break when actor Joshua Leonard was carrying it and rolled down a hill. However despite these unfortunate mistakes, there were many more happy accidents created by the unique shooting method.

POST-PRODUCTION

Editing and other post-production processes such as sound mixing are a critical stage in the production of any film. World renowned directors from Francis Ford Coppola to Martin Scorsese consider editing the essence of cinema. Even stars such as the late Philip Seymour Hoffman suggested that a film is made in the editing room, literally and metaphorically.

The actors in *The Blair Witch Project* may have taken almost sole responsibility for filming the footage but it is then up to the directors to cut the 20 hours of raw footage down into the length of a feature film. The importance of this process cannot be underestimated. What the directors selected for inclusion would determine how convincing the film would be to audiences. Myrick and Sánchez edited *The Blair Witch Project* themselves and had to select only what they deemed audiences would accept as true. Simultaneously they had to create a structured narrative that would appeal to horror movie fans who expect certain conventions from the genre.

From the 20 hours of footage, the directors sculpted the story and characterisations to suit their needs. Over eight months, Myrick and Sánchez made crucial decisions such as adding levity to the opening scenes and downplaying the conflict between Joshua and Heather, in order to build realistic character arcs that brought continuity and structure to the story.

The directors screened it for audiences, as is common in Hollywood filmmaking, in order to gain feedback and make changes that would ensure it appealed to as large an audience as possible. Comment cards were used to find out what audiences were responding well to and what they found scary.

At this point, the directors were still considering using the actors' footage as only a small part of the entire film. The hours and hours of footage shot in the woods was known by the directors as the 'Phase 1' footage. This would be edited together with 'Phase 2' footage that consisted of the backstory and would take the form of a more conventional mockumentary. However, after the directors spent eight months editing two different cuts (one from Myrick and one from Sánchez), they both decided the expositional Phase 2 footage was not working and decided to jettison it in favour of giving audiences 80 minutes of raw shaky-cam footage, almost completely captured by the actors.

This led to another bone of contention with the filmmakers of *The Last Broadcast*. Myrick and Sánchez had their rough cut complete featuring both Phase 1 and 2 footage and then 'on September 23rd, *indieWIRE*, a favourite magazine of the Haxan team, announced that the then little seen *The Last Broadcast* would be beamed digitally into art-house theatres as well as into 250,000 homes via the Independent Film Channel's broadband website during the next three months' according to Kendzior (1999: 39). Stefan Avalos, one of the directors of *The Last Broadcast*, says he is certain that it was at this point that the Haxan team changed their film after seeing *The Last Broadcast* and becoming aware that other people would see it. Avalos suggests the *Blair Witch* directors were worried audiences would think that *The Blair Witch Project* was a rip off, hence the decision to concentrate on the Phase 1 material. Avalos notes that the 'final version of *Blair*, stripped of the Phase II footage, no longer bears as great a resemblance to *Broadcast*' (1999: 39). In their defence, Myrick stated in an interview with Filmmaker magazine that 'when we started to plug it [the Phase II footage] in, it just took away from the heart of the "found" footage. We were fixing something that wasn't broken' (1999: 74).

After Artisan picked the film up for distribution, there was a budget for a professional sound mix and to shoot the alternate endings. In her article on *The Last Broadcast*, Sarah Kendzior even claims that the fact *Blair Witch* was chosen at Sundance is suspicious. She contends that *The Last Broadcast* 'was under serious consideration for a midnight showing at the Sundance Film Festival - until it was suddenly pulled at the last minute. *The Blair Witch Project* was screened in the same midnight spot one year later... Pierson, it should be noted, is a member of the Sundance selection committee' (1999: 38). The insinuation being that John Pierson, who had his own money in *The Blair Witch Project*, may well have been looking after his own interests by getting the film into Sundance at the expense of *The Last Broadcast*.

However, from there *The Blair Witch Project* began to outrun any criticism or controversy, as word of mouth began to take hold.

REFERENCES

Anon. (1999) 'An Exclusive Interview with Dan Myrick, Director of The Blair Witch Project.' *The House of Horror.* http://www.houseofhorrors.com/bwinterview.htm

Caro, M. (1999) 'Frightfully Frightfully, Frightfully Real: The Bewitching Story Behind 'The Blair Witch Project''. *Chicago Tribune.*

Gallagher, S. (1999) 'Into the Woods.' *Filmmaker.* 7 (2), 72-74.

Harris, M. (2001) 'The "Witchcraft" of Media Manipulation: Pamela and The Blair Witch Project.' *The Journal of Popular Culture.* 34 (4), 75-107.

Higley, S. L. and J. A. Weinstock (eds.) (2004) *Nothing That Is: Millennial Cinema and the Blair Witch Controversies.* Detroit: Wayne State University Press

Kaufman, A. (1999) 'Season of the Witch.' *The Village Voice.* http://www.villagevoice. com/1999-07-13/news/season-of-the-witch/

Kendzior, S. (1999) 'How The Last Broadcast Came First.' *Fangoria.* 188 (1), 36-39.

Klein, J. (1999) 'Interview: The Blair Witch Project.' *A.V. Club.* http://www.avclub.com/ articles/the-blair-witch-project,13607/

Lim, D. (1999) 'Heather Donahue Casts a Spell.' *The Village Voice.* http://www.villagevoice. com/1999-07-13/news/heather-donahue-casts-a-spell/

Mannes, B. (1999) 'Something Wicked.' *Salon.* http://www.salon.com/1999/07/13/witch_ actor/

McEnery, P. (1999) '"Blair Witch" Heather Found Alive.' *Getting It.com.* http://www. gettingit.com/article/693

Moore, R. (1999) 'America's Scariest Home Videos.' *Starburst.* 255 (1), 52-58.

Pincus, A. (1999) 'Off the Beaten Track: The Blair Witch Project.' *The Independent.* http:// www.independent-magazine.org/node/412

Young, J. (2009) '"The Blair Witch Project" 10 years later: Catching up with the directors of the horror sensation.' *Entertainment Weekly* http://popwatch.ew.com/2009/07/09/blair-witch/

2. THE AESTHETICS OF ARTIFICIAL AUTHENTICITY

The Blair Witch Project might at first glance appear to be a difficult film to talk about in terms of its visual style. After all how much can be said about a film that is so deliberately ugly with amateur camera work that it is said to have made audiences feel sick when watching it in cinemas? Actually, there is plenty to discuss as *The Blair Witch Project* is a very carefully constructed piece of fiction, deliberately crafted in terms of editing and cinematography to create the impression of authenticity.

In notable opposition to the slasher cycle that was revived with *Scream* and its progeny and the later 'torture porn' trend in modern horror, *The Blair Witch Project* takes a distinctively 'less is more' approach to visuals. It fails to reveal much that is horrific in the truest sense of excess that characterises much of the horror genre in film. There is none of the 'tits and gore' here for the stab happy slasher fans; *The Blair Witch Project* relies on the power of suggestion and the fear of what is unseen.

Following on from the shift in horror that occurred in the 1960s when horror went from something 'other' to being something within, *The Blair Witch Project* takes as realistic approach to the supernatural as it can possibly muster. After the Transylvanian vampires, gypsy werewolves and invading aliens of earlier horror, the genre shifted in the unsettling sixties and brought horror home. Films like *Night of the Living Dead*, *Last House on the Left*, *The Texas Chain Saw Massacre*, *The Exorcist* (1973) and later *Halloween* shifted the site of horror from somewhere foreign, dark and creepy to the very homes, streets and suburbs that much of the audience were from.

While *The Blair Witch Project* has a witch as the central antagonist and the dark and frightening woods as its primary location, it attempts to create a realistic atmosphere through its presentation, deceiving the viewer into thinking they are watching the actual found footage of three disappeared students. It is presented to the audience as a work of fact; not a traditional horror film, but a documentary chronicling real events that were filmed by someone involved in a terrible experience.

STYLISTIC INFLUENCES

The Blair Witch Project is influenced by the techniques and form of documentary filmmaking. It is adept at blurring the boundaries of fictional film and documentary by its adoption of the techniques, style and conventions of documentary film.

Documentaries and fiction films differ in terms of the level of control that the director has over what is happening in front of the camera. This makes for an interesting case study of the production of *The Blair Witch Project*. Bordwell and Thompson argue that 'the fiction film… is characterized by much more control over script and other aspects of the preparation and shooting phases' (1993: 29). As we have seen, in *The Blair Witch Project*, the characters/actors did the filming themselves with relatively little instruction or intrusion from the directors. Director Daniel Myrick said, 'realism being our prime directive, it necessitated us putting a camera in the actors' hands because that is what would be done, that's how it would be shot so we threw out convention' (McDowell, 2001: 144). The convention Myrick speaks of is of having a camera operator who is a professional and a part of the film's production crew. Actors do not conventionally shoot a film themselves. Therefore in some ways *The Blair Witch Project* is less of a fiction film than a documentary. The camera work and much of the script is improvised and therefore not fully dictated by directors and writers. This is unconventional for a fiction film and is clearly very influenced by, and displays many of the characteristics of, non-fiction filmmaking. The filmmakers might choose the setting and have a story they wish to tell (as with most documentary makers) but how exactly it is told and how the 'social actors' behave is more open and fluid.

The Blair Witch Project is also vitally influenced by the various international new wave movements of cinematic history such as Italian Neo-Realism and the French New Wave. Like these films, *The Blair Witch Project* is shot on location with handheld cameras and with the actors even using their own names. It is limited to natural lighting and much of the script is improvised. Neo-realism challenged the traditional ways of actors performing their roles by attempting to cast people who would 'be' rather than 'act' the parts. Attempts to get the actors to be scared rather than to act scared can clearly be seen in the filmmaking techniques employed by directors Myrick and Sánchez. Although the non-professional actors may not simply be the filmmaker characters of the narrative, they are to an extent 'being' scared as opposed to acting scared thanks to the real directors' method techniques. The contemporary acceptance of handheld camera work amongst film audiences can be traced back to the frequent use of it by New Wave filmmakers. *The Blair Witch Project* is itself intoxicated with the freedom provided by the handheld camera with characters that roam and run freely while filming.

At the same time that Italian Neo-realist films were appearing, the American film noir *The Lady in the Lake* (1947) was released. This film is a notable antecedent of *The Blair Witch Project* as, with only a few exceptions, the entire film is shot as if from the point-of-view of the protagonist. In The New York Times review of the film, it is stated 'YOU [sic] do get into the story and see things pretty much the way the protagonist, Phillip Marlowe, does, but YOU don't have to suffer the bruises he does. Of course, YOU don't get a chance to put your arms around Audrey Totter either. After all, the movie makers, for all their ingenuity, can go just so far in the quest for realism' (Pryor, 1947). This anticipates the appeal and critical reaction to films like *The Blair Witch Project*. Screenwriter John Swetnam says of found footage films that it 'just makes sense for horror because it puts you in the shoes of the story. You get to experience those scares in a more visceral and direct way' (Frappier, 2012). While the protagonist of *The Lady in the Lake* is not carrying his own diegetic camera and the audience is not witnessing the supposed footage filmed by him, the position of the spectator is constantly aligned with the position of the character.

Cinéma vérité is the form of documentary that combines many of the naturalistic techniques of Nichols' (2001) 'observational mode' with more intrusive and stylised techniques. The camera is often used to provoke subjects and the interaction of filmmaker and subject is seen as a method of increasing the perceived realism of the situation. The observational documentary route to realism attempted to make subjects feel as though they were not being filmed and also tried to make audiences feel they were witnessing real life, edited very little and presented as it was filmed. The filmmakers of cinéma vérité instead recognised that subjects will likely always be aware of the camera's presence and therefore, the documentary would be more real if it drew attention to this. The camera and documentary makers' presence should be noticeable to the viewer as it creates a different sense of realism where viewers are more aware that what they are watching is a construction. Audience awareness of the assembly of the film makes them more transparent and therefore arguably more real.

Certain fiction films adopted many of the cinéma vérité techniques to aid in their creation of realism. Though this adopting of these practices is not a new phenomenon, its significance to *The Blair Witch Project* cannot be understated. Like other films influenced by vérité techniques, it attempts to deny its status as fiction through its marketing. The producers attempt to deceive the public about the veracity of the events depicted in the film. This deception, as well as the formal qualities of the film, can be attributed to the filmmakers' desire to provoke strong responses to the film. As audiences, and particularly horror fans, have become more and more accepting of on screen violence, horror filmmakers have looked for new ways to scare and shock their audiences. Giving the viewer the uncanny sense that what they are seeing could be real footage of death and torture takes horror film watching into new and exciting territory for many fans of the genre.

In an interview with McDowell (2001: 141), Daniel Myrick concedes that 'the basic idea was those old documentaries; those old "*In Search of*" episodes that came on in the 70s'. *In Search of...* was a series that ran from 1977 to 1982 and in each episode a controversial or paranormal subject was investigated. There are numerous television precedents for its use of reality TV tropes to increase its sense of authenticity. Castonguay (2004: 66) notes that *The Blair Witch Project* includes documentary conventions but also considers reality TV to be one of the most important contextual factors for understanding the film.

Authenticity is a key factor that both reality TV and audiences of *The Blair Witch Project* desire. Signifiers of the 'real' are important in maintaining a sense of authenticity and to a contemporary audience, an awareness of the camera's presence is increasingly an important part of creating the 'reality' effect. The audience is conscious that the footage is not real life, but is also attentive to the fact that a camera operator was present in the diegesis. This is clear from the reaction of the operator to the scene that they witness.

The juxtaposition of individual to-camera confessions being edited next to footage of group discussions in reality television programmes such as *Big Brother* can also be seen in the film. With its diary room confessions cut together with the action in public living spaces, shows like *Big Brother* give audiences a look at group dynamics, but also more

Alone and terrified, Heather confesses her sins on the final night.

intimate access to individual members and their thoughts. *The Blair Witch Project* has an element of this technique with footage of the three students arguing with each other in a group contrasting with the confessional diary-cam moments of Heather crying and talking directly to the camera, alone and terrified in her tent at night. This means that, like reality TV, the viewer gets a privileged look at the group dynamics but also the very revealing personal insights and feelings of specific characters.

Another sub-genre of reality TV with an impact on *The Blair Witch Project* is what West (2005) calls 'caught-on-tape' TV. Like *The Blair Witch Project*, these shows use footage where spontaneous, aberrant and random events are captured. This can most clearly be seen where the actors/camera operators were put into improvisational situations where the directors were taunting them in the middle of the night by making noises and placing objects outside their tent. This meant that the responses of the protagonists are close to the genuine responses of amateur handy cam operators who capture the kind of footage that ends up on 'caught-on-tape' reality television. Camerawork that registers shock, confusion and fear is imitated in the cinematography of *The Blair Witch Project* as it captures both the surprise of the camera operators as well as spontaneous and shocking unscripted events.

Some criticisms of *The Blair Witch Project* have centred on its slow pace, repetitiveness and lack of a tightly scripted narrative structure and dialogue. A further comparison can be made with much of reality television. The characters in *The Blair Witch Project* argue relentlessly and traipse around in circles in woods that offer no differing *mise-en-scène* for much of the film but this again heightens the realism. Higley (2004: 101) amusingly suggests '*BWP* gives American viewers what they liked in "reality TV," a voyeuristic glimpse of people on the edge screaming at one another'.

Another antecedent is the Dogme 95 manifesto, written by Danish directors Lars von Trier and Thomas Vinterberg. It consists of a set of filmmaking rules that would foreground story and acting and exclude using elaborate technology and special effects. While all ten rules of the manifesto are not adhered to by *The Blair Witch Project*, there are many rules that are. Location shooting, diegetic sound only, hand-held camera and only natural lighting, as well as the tendency for improvised dialogue and camerawork can all be seen in both films of the Dogme 95 movement such as von Trier's *The Idiots* (1998) and *The Blair Witch Project*.

There are clear parallels between the shooting styles of films like *Breaking the Waves* (1996) and *The Blair Witch Project* where the camera work feels improvised and spontaneous. Instead of using a crew to film *The Blair Witch Project*, the actors playing the diegetic characters held the cameras and filmed the scenes themselves. The directors would not be present on location with them and therefore all camerawork and the majority of dialogue is completely improvised. Therefore this spontaneous camera action adds to the authenticity of the images. It also aids identification with the characters as many camera movements reveal how the characters are feeling; their shock at an unexpected noise, for example. These genuine moments of the camera operator's surprise being reflected by the camera movements can also be seen in films of the Dogme 95 movement where the camera operators also did not always know what to expect in a scene.

THE SHOCK OF THE MOCK-DOC

Primarily, *The Blair Witch Project* begins as a mockumentary or mock-documentary.

Hight (2001) defines mockumentaries (or mock-documentaries) as 'media texts... which "look" and/or "sound" like documentaries or reality-based media... fictional texts which appropriate the aesthetics of the documentary genre or other reality-based media'. Their use of documentary conventions was generally used for comedic purposes in the past with classic examples like *This is Spinal Tap* (1984) ruthlessly parodying the stars and conventions of rockumentaries and later ones like *Borat: Cultural Learnings of America for Make Benefit Glorious Nation of Kazakhstan* (2006) not only tricking their audiences but also duping the general public into becoming unwitting extras in the film.

The mockumentary uses conventions of the documentary mode such as interviews, natural lighting and handheld camera to deceive the viewer into believing the text to be a work of fact, not fiction. *Cannibal Holocaust* had previously used this approach in the horror genre by presenting a documentary film within the fiction film. Different to *The Blair Witch Project*, much of the narrative is concerned with the search for the film shot by some documentary makers who have gone missing in the Amazonian jungle. However, then the film switched to showing the contents of the film canisters found in the jungle and this footage is presented in the mockumentary style.

The Blair Witch Project eliminates the search and discovery of the tapes shot by the three filmmakers and instead presents only what they shot to the audience. There is no framing device, only a supposedly real document of what the characters witnessed and experienced. However, *The Blair Witch Project* is not simply a mockumentary. What begins as an earnest effort to create a documentary by Heather and her crew quickly descends into what is closer to fake cinéma vérité. All attempts at objectivity, formal presenting and interview techniques are lost in favour of raw, seemingly uncut footage where Heather provokes her subjects by continually filming them.

There are none of the traditional cues that tell an audience that they are watching a Hollywood fiction film; even the marketing claimed the truthfulness of the events depicted. There is no music, no establishing shots and no stars to take the audience on a safe, continuity edited filmic adventure. The distinction between documentary and fiction is so blurred that the film is much more likely to have a stronger impact on audiences than recognisable horror genre fodder.

Many films in the past, including *Cannibal Holocaust*, have used genuine documentary footage in their narratives to provide what Black (2002: 12) calls a 'kernel of truth' to create a core of authenticity that the rest of the film can utilise to appear more reliable. However *The Blair Witch Project* contains no such 'kernels of truth' and still manages to seem authentic, arguably beyond any other horror film in history. The whole film appears to be a documentary artefact but in fact has no truth to it at all with the exception of a few genuine town locals being interviewed on camera and ending up in the film. Yet even these locals are unwittingly talking about a fabricated myth.

What makes *The Blair Witch Project* seem so real, is that it is constructed unlike a normal fiction film. The audience of Classical Hollywood narrative fictions is encouraged to forget that they are watching a film. Feature film principles such as seamless editing and unself-conscious camerawork, actors that ignore the presence of the camera and well-lit and composed shots that draw the viewer into the world of the film to watch what is going on in the diegesis as a silent, invisible observer are not present here. Oddly for a film that claims to be real, the audience is constantly reminded that this is a film, a representation and a mediation of events that have already occurred. But the reason we believe what we see more in *The Blair Witch Project* than in other horror films is precisely because of our trust in cameras and recorded footage. Though we are acutely aware that this is a film and a construction, the spectator is also invited to believe what they see on screen. These characters went into the woods and captured it for themselves; this footage is the proof of what they witnessed. Recording media like video cameras do not lie; they capture what is filmed, vividly and resembling real life.

Directors Daniel Myrick and Eduardo Sánchez deliberately construct the visuals of *The Blair Witch Project* to deceive the viewer into believing what they see is real footage. Though *The Blair Witch Project* contains no special effects in terms of CGI and only one instance of blood and gore, the film is itself one long special effect from start to finish. By declining to use the latest in high tech special effects wizardry and instead focussing on creating a plausible piece of 'documentary' footage, the directors made their film seem infinitely more real than many other horror films. The attempts of some horror films to out-do each other with increasing levels of realistic gore, created through computer generated and practical effects, might make the films look real but it does not necessarily make them *feel* real.

Whereas modern techniques could have been used to create a grim, disturbing and captivating depiction of a witch in the woods, The Blair Witch Project takes a far more minimalist approach that complements the mockumentary format. The fact that the visuals only ever imply the presence of a supernatural force and never consolidate what we suspect and fear by revealing an actual presence, ultimately aids the audience in accepting what is being suggested, much more than if we were to have our predictions and hypotheses confirmed. The subtlety in the portrayal of the supernatural is vital to the illusion of realism. Both the mock-documentary aesthetics and the lack of proof of what is haunting the filmmakers in the woods enhances the verisimilitude and helps spectators to accept what they see as truth.

The mockumentary format also primes the viewer 'for acceptance of low-budget production values' (Aloi, 2005: 191). Horror films often have lower budgets as they are traditionally made for a niche audience of genre fans and adult viewers, with their age rating classifications often restricting the audience significantly. Audiences assume that documentaries will have lower quality visuals due to their similarly low budgets and often improvised shooting methods. As in reality television and documentary, The Blair Witch Project shows signs of spontaneous camerawork and there are likely to be some technical imperfections that come with the form. These have to be created by the filmmakers deliberately in order to convince viewers of the authentic qualities of the footage. They also allow the directors to make a horror film where the low budget serves the horror, and does not need to be hidden or masked from the audience.

CINEMATOGRAPHY AND MISE-EN-SCÈNE

The cinematography of The Blair Witch Project is characterised as being crafted by what Ingle (2011) calls a 'diegetic camera'. If the diegesis is the 'world of the film', then the diegetic camera is simply a camera that exists within the world of the film. It is not an invisible observer capturing the action as in most fiction films, but is instead part of the action. The characters can hold it, see it and speak to it. Therefore the camera is either being held by a character in the story or has been deliberately set up by a character in the story. Though the camera is often positioned at the eye of the operator, the diegetic camera differs slightly to the subjective camera of traditional films. Ingle states that 'the subjective camera differs from the diegetic camera in that while the subjective camera reveals the point of view of a character, it is not shot by a character, nor it is acknowledged'. So while we see from Michael Myers' point of view in the extended opening shot of seminal slasher *Halloween* and his sister does indeed address Michael by looking into the subjective camera, the character is not acknowledging the presence of the camera but rather the presence of the character with whose point of view we in the audience have been temporarily aligned. Therefore the camerawork of *The Blair Witch Project* is often made up of point of view shots but these are different to the point of view, subjective shots of traditional cinematic experiences.

There are two diegetic cameras in *The Blair Witch Project*, one mainly being operated by Heather and the other mostly by Josh. Heather has a Hi8 video camera that captures colour footage and Josh films on the bigger and more professional 16mm film black and white camera. The distinction between the uses of both cameras is most noticeable in the early scenes before the characters dispose of the idea of making a formal documentary and begin filming their own descent into bickering and terror. The video camera is used to capture the more private and behind the scenes style footage whereas Josh uses the 16mm camera to capture the official documentary footage for the intended audience of their project.

The jerky camera movement, hesitant pans, shaky tracking and often wild actions of the camera are all down to the camera operating characters. While some of the cinematography appears slightly more professional and staged, other parts look like the work of an amateur who is putting little (if any) thought into framing and composition. Either way, the audience is constantly reminded of the camera's presence, and therefore to some extent, of the artificiality of what they are watching. The paradox is that this awareness of the camera and the representational nature of what is being shown enhances the realism as spectators trust the camera not to lie. We are also more inclined to believe what we see due to the amateur nature of the footage. The inexperience of the camera operators and their basic and limited techniques emphasise that the footage must be real and is not polished and carefully crafted enough to be faked.

One of the greatest assets of constructing the cinematography in this way is that all this shakiness, poor framing and lack of focus implies much about not only Heather or Josh or whoever is holding the camera's state of mind, but also it strongly suggests that the spectator is not seeing everything. The camera often appears to miss things, its swift movement implying a quickened response of the operator but also the idea that perhaps there is something off camera that moves quicker than the operator can react to. It makes for hyperrealism as the footage appears immediate and visceral, but lacking in concrete evidence of supernatural occurrences in the woods. Schopp (2004: 137) suggests there is a relationship between immediacy and obscurity in that the less the audience actually gets to see, the greater their desire for proof and the more immediate and intense the experience of watching becomes.

Another essential tool in obscuring what the viewer and the characters can see is lighting. *The Blair Witch Project* features completely naturalistic lighting. If a scene takes place during the night, then it really is pitch black except for what the light on the camera can pick up. The viewer is again in exactly the same position as the characters because if they cannot see, then we cannot see. The use of a camera light could be considered a cinematic tool as lighting is usually considered an essential part of the cinematography that gives a film its distinctive look. However the scenes where the light is required in *The Blair Witch Project* are anything but traditionally cinematic. They are frustrating, unclear, poorly lit and the light source comes from within the diegesis but is of little use to the characters. This natural lighting is reminiscent of many documentaries and therefore fits the mockumentary format of the film and is also an essential part of the power of the narrative. The darkness is blacker than in most horror movies and therefore the lack of knowledge of what is in the woods and outside their tent at night is all the more terrifying for the characters and the audience.

Horror films have always played on peoples' fear of the dark but rarely have they really made the most of the genre's most significant visual convention. Horror films fail to show the true darkness as they have to conform to fiction film conventions of allowing the audience to be able to see clearly what is happening on screen. Myrick and Sánchez's use of the darkness is total and uncompromising. The single light source adds little clarity to the surroundings and fails to illuminate what horrors await the characters. They reinvent the horror genre by reminding us why we fear the dark; because we cannot see what is right in front of us let alone what is outside our tent as we camp alone in the woods, miles from civilisation.

Using the darkness to its fullest also privileges sound over visuals. If the dark is all encompassing then other senses become more important to the viewers and the characters. The sounds are what wake Heather, Josh and Mike in the middle of the night. Distant cries, strange sounds and twigs snapping are all signifiers of something out there but the darkness never allows them or us to see what is causing these sounds. It is a terror born of blindness but exacerbated by the elusive and mysterious sounds that can be vaguely heard.

Darkness is not the only thing that restricts our vision and the cinematography of *The Blair Witch Project* is also used to limit what the viewer can see by aligning us mostly with the point of view of the character holding the camera. Unlike in many other films where the omniscient camera can be anywhere, with any characters at any time and the director can show us scenes happening in different places and involving other characters apart from the protagonists, *The Blair Witch Project* limits our experience of the narrative to that of the experience of the central three characters. There are no aerial shots to show how far the protagonists are from civilisation, no parallel edited scenes to show the witch preparing her cunning plans to taunt the young filmmakers and no cutaways to their worried families back at home. We are limited to spending the entire running time with the protagonists, and their point of view is almost exactly the same as our point of view throughout.

Where *The Blair Witch Project* also differs from its predecessors in the horror genre is in its use of the subjective camera. While *The Blair Witch Project* has camera work that is aligned with the point of view of a character, it is not exactly the same as the subjective camera of traditional films for the reasons outlined earlier. *The Blair Witch Project* is also interesting for putting audiences in the viewpoint of the victims rather than the monster. In slasher films of the 1980s cycle, the audience is often positioned with the subjective viewpoint of the monster as s/he lurks in the woods watching his victims as they obliviously smoke, drink, take drugs, skinny dip and have sex. Audiences at the time were known to cheer on the monsters as they ploughed their way through the disposable teen cast but the cinematography here forces us into identification not with the monster but with the victims. This makes the audience more anxious than if they were willing the monster to succeed so they can get their next dose of murder and mutilation.

The use of real locations is a central focus of the *mise-en-scène* with the wooded location being clearly real. There is no sense of this being a constructed set or that the filmmakers have even designed their production except for the creepy stickmen and rock bundles that appear in the woods to freak out the characters. Everything on screen is real and natural; from the forest, to the characters and their costumes and make up. Heather is far from the stereotypical Final Girl in appearance. She is dressed for comfort; not style, sexiness or to show off her figure and beauty. Similarly the guys are not the buffed up, plastic looking men of recent horror remakes but resemble ordinary students, bundled up warm for the cold nights ahead and completely identifiable as young filmmakers working on a low budget. None are heroes or villains; they are just scared young people with flaws that all help to get them killed.

The woods are recognisable horror iconography from fairytales like *Hansel and Gretel* to Camp Crystal Lake to the recent *Mama* (2013). They are a symbol of the natural world and a place in which it is easy to become lost. They are dark and unforgiving; far removed from civilisation and a reminder of the savagery of the past. The repetitive *mise-en-scène* of the trees, the river and the lack of human intervention are a permanent reminder of the characters' helplessness. After Josh's disappearance, Heather and Josh are Hansel and Gretel, lost without their bread crumb trail and forced to confront the witch in her house deep in the forest, a perverse symmetry with the film's opening sequence. Heather is introduced in her bedroom and the characters move from the safety and comfort of their homes and families outwards into the unknown of the forest as pointedly shown by the shot of Josh's car as they walk away from it and it gets smaller as they grow more distant, getting deeper into the woods.

The haunted house, another trusty staple of the traditional horror movie emerges as if out of nowhere for the climax of the film. As explained in the surrounding mythology, this is Rustin Parr's house. Parr was the killer of children who heard voices and made his victims stand facing the wall as he killed other victims. This is the most designed element of the *mise-en-scène* of the film. Small handprints cover the walls; a cable looks almost like a noose but the grubby, run-down interior is not the safe haven Heather and Mike hope for. It is the place of their presumed deaths and the site where their footage is later found buried. It is less grand than the gothic mansions of old haunted house stories but it is in keeping with the rest of the film, more realistic and infinitely more terrifying.

EDITING

The editing of The Blair Witch Project is interesting because it draws attention to itself, but also aims to hide the fact that what is being watched is an edited version of the raw footage that was supposedly found. The words at the start of the film just say 'their footage was found' and there is no mention of it having been edited down into a coherent narrative. However, from the early scenes it becomes obvious that editing has taken place. The cross cutting of the footage of the two cameras as Josh and Heather film each other is the earliest evidence that the audience is not simply seeing all of the footage out of one camera and then all of the footage from the other. The mixing of 'behind the scenes' footage with the 'official document' seems to suggest that we are seeing everything but there is clear evidence that some unknown figure has cut together the footage and most likely cut it down to fit feature length.

Documentaries and therefore also mockumentaries are often less fluid in their editing. The spontaneous nature of capturing 'real life' often means that shots cannot be snipped as carefully and seamlessly as in fiction feature films. The Blair Witch Project features jump cuts and flash frames, which draw attention to the edited nature of the material. At some points tension is heightened when the editor chooses to leave some shots lasting for just a little longer than is comfortable for the audience. These are moments edited to emphasise the drama of the narrative and are clearly not the product of being simply shown the rushes of what was shot. Close to 20 hours of footage were captured and the finished film is 87 minutes long so it is clear that a huge amount of editing has taken place. What is particularly effective about the editing of The Blair Witch Project is how the editing gives the audience a sense of seeing everything that was shot while actually being a very carefully constructed film in the tradition of narrative filmmaking.

Heather and Josh film one another but who edited the footage together?

SELF-CONSCIOUSNESS

Another facet of the aesthetics of *The Blair Witch Project*, its self-consciousness, is tied into its mockumentary approach, its point of view camera and its often obvious editing. It is a self-reflexive text, meaning it is a film about filmmaking. It refers to its own construction and the characters in the film are completely aware that they are on camera and a part of a film. Though the audience is watching a fiction film, the characters believe they are making and starring in their own documentary that turns into more of an amateur video about them getting lost in the woods.

For this reason, *The Blair Witch Project* resembles metafiction. This is where a text reminds the reader or viewer that they are watching or reading a fiction. It draws attention to itself as a construction and in the case of a metafiction film, never lets the viewer forget that what they are watching is a film. So Heather, Josh and Mike are constantly aware that they are making a film. This is the strange paradox that both makes *The Blair Witch Project* more and less realistic at the same time. It is further confounded by the self-conscious *mise-en-scène* of having the characters look and talk directly to the camera, and by extension the audience. The footage contained in *The Blair Witch Project* breaks a fundamental rule of cinema in that the characters gaze directly into the camera and this means that again, realism is both heightened and lost.

The characters' gaze tells us they see the camera and acknowledge it and even discuss its use but it also takes us out of the position of invisible observer. Mike might shout at Heather for keeping the camera rolling, but when we are in the point of view of Heather, Mike also shouts at us. It takes us out of the comfortable position of spectator and forces us on location as a helpless observer.

The *mise-en-scène* of the film, and the many surrounding artefacts such as the promotional website and the accompanying mock-documentary, *The Curse of the Blair Witch*, attempt to convince audiences of the verisimilitude of the Blair Witch myth. Meanwhile, the self-consciousness simultaneously draws attention to the artifice. Having characters that look directly at the camera is rejecting a vital convention of realism but by doing this, Myrick and Sánchez actually conversely create more realism. This is due to the blurring of boundaries between the film as fiction, and the film as mockumentary. Audiences do accept that the people on screen in TV news reports, home movies and many documentaries do acknowledge the presence of the camera and directly address it, and therefore these moments sit comfortably in *The Blair Witch Project*.

VISUAL EFFECTS AND VISUAL AFFECTS

There are numerous purposes for the aesthetic strategy of *The Blair Witch Project*. The desire of every horror filmmaker to provoke strong responses in the audience is no different with Myrick and Sánchez's film. Whereas many horror films wish to incite disgust at the gore and feelings of horror at the terrifying images of a monster, *The Blair Witch Project*'s low budget production values have a 'less is more' approach. Arguably, they create more of a reaction than many other, more explicit examples of horror cinema.

The Blair Witch Project's visuals leave much to the viewer's imagination. The witch is never seen in the film and audiences are left to imagine what she looks like, if indeed they choose to accept that she even does exist in the diegesis. The audience is forced into evaluating that the witch probably does exist as something is definitely in these woods taunting Heather, Mike and Josh. There are many clues to suggest that a supernatural entity is responsible. The construction of the witch is left very much to our imaginations.

Our visualisations must be created by our own minds and therefore the witch may look completely different to different viewers. Active spectatorship is enforced as opposed to a more passive experience where the filmmakers have a very strict preferred reading. Though interviewees near the start of the film refer to a mist rising out of the river and a woman completely covered in hair, the reality of the film's villain could be anything we want it to be. We can project our worst fears or our previous experience of movie witches onto the antagonist. She can look like whatever fearful picture our imaginations can conjure. Or she can remain a frightening blank, never to be filled.

The fact that we never see the woman once known as Elly Kedward also makes our imaginations work harder to fill in the blanks of what we are not seeing. Like the use of the dark in the night scenes, the viewer is forced to visualise what they cannot see. The distant sounds of crying outside their tents could be anything and our minds must create answers for the questions posed by the lack of light. This means that rather than having a specific shock or object-directed scare like we have when a slasher villain like Freddy or Jason pops out from behind a tree, in The Blair Witch Project there is no clear and visible object for us to be scared of. It creates an overriding sense of dread, unease and anxiety that lasts for the majority of the film with the intention of staying with us for a long time after. Matt Hills (2005: 26) argues that having no clearly defined object to be fearful of causes 'affective saturation'. The viewer's mood and emotions throughout the film are guided by this overriding sensation of unease, or what Hills (2005: 27) calls 'objectless anxiety'. Like in many traditional slasher films where the supposedly killed villain's body vanishes in the final frames, leaving the audience with the sense that the evil could still be out there, The Blair Witch Project similarly leaves us with the impression the witch still haunts the woods and not only that, but we also have no way of knowing what she looks like.

This engages our imaginations and is intended to make the fear last long after the film finishes. The mockumentary format also aims to disrupt the idea of narrative safety. Whereas other films are clearly recognisable as fiction, The Blair Witch Project attempts to convince us it is real footage. It puts us in the 'documentary mode of engagement' (Tresca, 2011), convincing us that what we are about to watch is real and that we should read it as such. When the supernatural elements are suggested, it undermines the reality of the footage. By never making anything obvious or using special effects or giving us a clear look at the witch, the viewer cannot discount the potential veracity of the footage. Usually a spectator can distance themselves from anything too scary in a film by repeating the mantra used to sell Wes Craven's *Last House on the Left*, 'Keep telling yourself it's only a movie'. By positioning the audience to expect a documentary experience, early viewers of *The Blair Witch Project* would have narrative safety disrupted, making it much more difficult for them to see it as 'only a movie'.

A final idea to consider about the effect of the aesthetics of *The Blair Witch Project* is that different audiences will respond in different ways. The idea that some people were convinced they were seeing a real documentary when the film was first screened at Sundance is dubious, though there must have been those unsure of exactly *what* they were seeing. Their responses must have been much stronger if they had genuine doubts over the veracity of the footage. Also, some audience members were said to feel nauseous at the shaky camera work but younger viewers raised on the aesthetics of reality television and the increasing use of handheld camera work in TV and film would no doubt be far more used to this cinematography and would not feel quite so disoriented by it. If the pleasure of horror films is primarily to be scared, then the film has succeeded in no small part due to the effects of its visuals on the audience.

REFERENCES

Aloi, P. (2005) 'Beyond the Blair Witch: a new horror aesthetic?' In: King, G. (ed.) *The Spectacle of the Real: from Hollywood to reality TV and beyond*. Bristol: Intellect.

Black, J. (2002) *The Reality Effect: film culture and the graphic imperative*. London: Routledge

Bordwell, D. and Thompson, K. (1993) *Film art: an introduction*. Palatino: Ruttle, Shaw & Wetherill, Inc.

Castonguay, J. (2004) 'The political economy of the indie blockbuster: fandom, intermediality, and The Blair Witch Project' In: Higley, S. L. and J. A. Weinstock (eds) (2004) *Nothing That Is: Millennial Cinema and the Blair Witch Controversies*. Detroit: Wayne State University Press

Frappier, R. (2012) 'Interview: why are found footage movies so popular?' Available from: http://screenrant.com/popular-found-footage-movies-robf-154762/ [Accessed 14th November 2012]

Hight, C. (2001) 'Mockumentary: Reflexivity, satire and a call to play.' Available from: http://www.waikato.ac.nz/film/mock-doc.shtml [Accessed 11th June]

Higley, S. (2004) '"People just want to see something": art, death, and document in Blair Witch, The Last Broadcast, and Paradise Lost' In: Higley, S. L. and J. A. Weinstock (eds) (2004) Nothing That Is: Millennial Cinema and the Blair Witch Controversies. Detroit: Wayne State University Press

Hills, M. (2005) The Pleasures of Horror. London: Continuum

Ingle, Z. (2011) George A. Romero's Diary of the Dead and the rise of the Diegetic Camera in Recent Horror Films. OI3Media Available from: http://host.uniroma3.it/riviste/OI3Media/Ingle.html

McDowell, S. D. (2001) 'Method filmmaking: an interview with Daniel Myrick, co-director of The Blair Witch Project', Journal of Film and Video, 53:2/3, pp. 140-7

Nichols, B. (2001) Introduction to documentary. Bloomington: Indiana University Press

Pryor, T. (1947) Lady in the Lake (1946) At the Capitol. Available from: http://movies.nytimes.com/movie/review?res=9C04E3DE123EEE3BBC4C51DFB766838C659EDE [Accessed 30th June 2012]

Schopp, A. (2004) 'Transgressing the safe space: Generation X horror in The Blair Witch Project and Scream' In: Higley, S. L. and J. A. Weinstock (eds) (2004) Nothing That Is: Millennial Cinema and the Blair Witch Controversies. Detroit: Wayne State University Press

Tresca, D. (2011) 'Lying to Reveal the Truth: Horror Pseudo-Documentaries and the Illusion of Reality.' OI3Media Available from: http://host.uniroma3.it/riviste/OI3Media/Tresca.html

West, A. (2005) 'Caught on tape: a legacy of low-tech reality' In: King, G. (ed.) The Spectacle of the Real: from Hollywood to reality TV and beyond. Bristol: Intellect.

3. WHO AM I? POSITIONING THE SPECTATOR AND IDENTIFICATION

One of the primary reasons for the continued use of the found footage aesthetic, popularised in *The Blair Witch Project*, must be that it increases identification for horror film viewers. These fans of the horror genre search for films that will terrify them. Having a character hold a camera is the closest a spectator can get to living the film, but they get to experience it from the safety of their seat in front of the screen. Considering the positioning of spectators, and exploring the cognitive processes that lead to increased identification, is essential. Is it really as simple as suggesting that, because the cameras are in the hands of the characters, audiences will identify more with them, and therefore be more scared? Many film theorists have considered identification, empathy and emotion and some have applied their findings to *The Blair Witch Project*. However, there is room for further exploration of the most potent reasons behind the use of the aesthetics discussed in the previous chapter.

The Blair Witch Project is unlike many slasher films that are known to encourage identification with the murderers. It is instead a film that rejects the idea of understanding or empathising with killers and as an alternative, encourages strong identification with the victim characters. The idea of being trapped in the narrative of the victims, and particularly the perspective of two/three characters, will now be explored in relation to identification. It is also important to consider how this concept can be problematic when the cameras can switch hands between characters.

Finally this chapter will explore the pleasure of this kind of identification, and the idea that audiences wish to experience the action in a visceral way, without actually giving up their safety. *The Blair Witch Project* attempts to disrupt the safety of the viewing experience and unlike a first-person videogame, leaves the viewer with no control over the characters' actions.

As far back as the First World War there is a precedent for subjective camerawork like in *The Blair Witch Project*, seen in some cases of war reporting. The imperilled characters of *The Blair Witch Project*, that cling to cameras in the face of their imminent deaths, can be seen as the spiritual descendants of the war reporter cameramen who put themselves in dangerous situations to capture extraordinary events. The footage is of real events, not staged for the camera and the audience is aware that a camera operator was present to capture the on screen events as they happened. The tension between knowing a camera operator is in danger and knowing that the moment of capture has passed is also present in *The Blair Witch Project*.

In *Filming Death*, Balasz (1945: 31) discusses a war film where a cameraman is killed but the film continues as the camera still records. This kind of sequence does not actually depict a real death on the screen but suggests it through the overturning of the camera. In *The Blair Witch Project*'s infamous final frames, Heather runs into a room of an old house and the audience is left to imagine what happens to her as the camera drops to the ground on its side. Nothing appears on screen to suggest what might have caused the camera operator to drop the camera or fall over with the camera, but the silence that follows her screams implies that she is no longer capable of filming.

The Blair Witch Project is also influenced by the idea of a camera operator who refuses to stop filming even when faced with imminent threat. Josh and Mike repeatedly chastise Heather for continually recording when they are clearly in an increasingly dangerous situation. This is not only a realistic depiction of a character that does not wish to be filmed under stressful circumstances but also gives Heather opportunities to voice her reasoning for why she is still filming in such extreme circumstances. The protagonists argue over the continual use of the camera but at the climax of the film, as Heather and Mike run around the old house in the woods in search of Josh, they are both still recording what they see until the moment of their disappearance. No matter how hard it is to believe that the character would still be filming under the circumstances they find themselves in, *The Blair Witch Project* makes it easy to identify with Heather. At one point, she says that recording is 'all she has left'. Both the war reporters of the past who lost their lives while filming, and also the construction of Heather's character as determined and stubborn, make it easy for spectators to relate to her desire to keep filming. Particularly in an age of vloggers, social media and selfies, audiences can relate to wanting to share their most exciting/dangerous experiences via a camera with others.

Modern, cheap cameras that are small and easy to hold and manoeuvre do tend to produce a lower quality of image. However they can also tell the viewer more about the person holding the camera. These small handheld devices register the movement of the operator which increases the identification a viewer feels with the camera operator. The lack of tripod usage means that the viewer gets a better sense of the movement and therefore potentially the state-of-mind of the operator. As previously discussed, camcorders can record the emotions of the user. This is another key to understanding the pleasures of *The Blair Witch Project* for horror fans that wish to be terrified. Not only is what is on screen often horrific and terrifying, but the hand that records it is also terrified, frantic and out of control, giving the viewer even more reason to be afraid. It is a more visceral experience if the hand that controls the camera is itself lacking in control. When Heather and Josh run through the woods after being terrified in their tent at night, it is impossible to see the emotions on their faces. However, the screams and hectic camera movement perfectly suggest people that are running for their lives. Not allowing the viewer to see what is happening to the camera operator can also provoke fear in the viewer. If a character pans the camera quickly left to right, the viewer might wonder what has caused their swift movement. Therefore these modern, small and easily manoeuvrable cameras are essential to this style of filmmaking.

Though many will disregard *The Blair Witch Project* for its lack of traditional cinematographic or artistic style, it is precisely this that gives the film its power and draws the audience closer into the story and its characters. Packham (2012) suggests that this is 'a particularly effective approach in horror films, for which the desired emotional response is visceral'. While most movies encourage passivity in spectators and the safe awareness that 'it's only a movie', *The Blair Witch Project* challenges that notion by being presented very differently to the majority of other fiction films.

THEORIES OF IDENTIFICATION

The idea of identification is problematic and many film theorists have debated the term. What exactly does it means to identify with a character, and what techniques encourage this connection between the audience and character? Before exploring the notion of identification in relation to *The Blair Witch Project*, it is important to first consider the theory of identification and what exactly it entails.

Identification is a psychological term and a concept that is rooted in the writing of the founder of psychoanalysis, Sigmund Freud. It is the process where a person incorporates or assimilates some aspects or attributes of another person and is therefore transformed in some way to become more like the other that they have identified with.

In the 1970s, psychoanalytic film theorists such as Christian Metz and Laura Mulvey emphasised the idea of identification, stressing that spectators would identify with the camera's gaze and usually the (male) leading character. Metz and Mulvey both argued that the positioning of the camera, what it filmed and how it filmed it, all made viewers identify with its gaze. Mulvey influentially noted how the camera would often linger over the female star, encouraging the male spectator to share in the camera/director/male star's desire to stare at her beauty. The psychoanalytic model of identification roots spectators' desire for cinema and watching the image on screen with a sense of lack, or of something missing and a desire for completeness that they have harboured since birth (Metz, 1982).

Cognitive theorists such as David Bordwell and Noël Caroll have moved the discussion towards a fuller understanding of the processes of the mind that lead to identification. There has also been far more consideration of what exactly it means to identify with someone. Debating and often dismissing many of the ideas of the psychoanalytic theorists, cognitive film theorists interrogate the concept of identification as a complex process and many have come up with different ideas about how exactly it works. Identification is too broad a word for such a many faceted concept and ideas of empathy, sympathy, engagement and alignment must all be factored in to any discussion of the viewer's relationship with the characters on screen. It is essential to look at some of the critical theory that surrounds the issue of identification before discussing *The Blair Witch Project*.

NOËL CARROLL

Carroll (91: 1990) asserts that what many theorists have suggested is identifying with a character is 'emotional duplication' where the spectator feels the same as the character. Sometimes the fiction can be vivid enough to make us feel as though we are the protagonists. However Carroll also posits that there are many times when we in the audience feel something different to the character on screen, for example when we have more knowledge about a situation than the character does.

Carroll's theory has been criticised by many for being focused on object-directed emotions. Carroll often refers to how characters will feel when confronted with something to fear. His theory is based on the idea that in horror, both the characters and the audience feel fear because they see an object that is horrific. However *The Blair Witch Project* is interesting for never revealing its monster and for showing very little that could be considered a traditional cause for fear.

Carroll basically believes that identification is not as simple as sharing the same emotion as a character. What he believes that we do, instead of identifying with a character in a film, is assimilate their situation. When a film such as *The Blair Witch Project* puts us constantly in the point of view of a character, this assimilation should be more complete, and the experience will therefore be scarier. However, some have argued otherwise.

BERYS GAUT

Gaut (1999: 202) believes that identification is simply 'putting oneself in the character's shoes'. This idea is clearly exemplified by the audience being almost totally isolated in the point of view of one or more of the characters. The audience is positioned almost the entire way through the film in Heather, Mike or Josh's shoes and we see as if out of their eyes, or at least the camera that they hold to their eye. Gaut argues that viewers in the audience imagine being the character who they identify with. So if we identify with Heather as we see the footage from her camera most often, then we imagine what we would feel like in her situation, a task made easier by our positioning and restricting to her point of view.

MURRAY SMITH

Smith's (1995: 73) theory of identification breaks the notion down into three different concepts: 'recognition, alignment, and allegiance'. He calls these constituent parts of the

Mike admits to kicking the map into the creek. The audience chooses to identify with Heather and Josh.

structure of sympathy. Sympathy is similar to empathy in that it is the sharing of feelings between people but often it is also used to describe a feeling of sorrow or distress for another person.

Firstly, Smith asserts that we must recognise and perceive the construction of a character. Despite being positioned in the point of view of Heather, Mike and Josh for much of *The Blair Witch Project*, the audience still gets to see images of each. Even when they are not on screen, we can often hear them as well, so we are aware of a continuous human presence throughout the film. According to Murray, the next stage in the structure is alignment. This is the process of placing the spectators in a position where they have access to certain actions, knowledge and feelings of the characters. A key moment in *The Blair Witch Project* occurs when Mike admits he has kicked the map into the creek. Though we never see Heather in this scene, we hear her hysterical shouting and screaming at Mike and her feelings are made perfectly clear. Finally, allegiance is where spectators will make moral evaluations about the characters and choose whether they will identify with them or not. Again, in this same scene, it is much easier to identify with Heather and Josh as they attack Mike because the average viewer will consider the problem to be Mike's fault.

ALEX NEILL

Neill highlights the importance of empathy in the process of identifying with a fictional character. Empathy is the intellectual identification with or vivid experience of another person or character's feelings, thoughts, or attitudes. Empathy suggests something beyond simply feeling the same emotions as someone else but also a distinct cognitive process that allows someone to actively engage with how another person is feeling.

Neill (1996: 183) suggests that identification and empathy depend on a viewer's ability to imagine what the character's beliefs and desires might be. Without detailed knowledge about the character, it will be harder for the spectator to imagine things from their point of view. Neill's argument also considers the similarities between the person in the audience and the character on screen. He suggests that the greater extent to which the character is like the viewer, the more the viewer will be able to imagine events from the character's point of view. For example, a young female documentary filmmaker might be able to identify with Heather more than a middle aged male doctor. Similarly, the three characters will be similar in terms of age and ethnicity as the target audience. Furthermore, a viewer with experience of filmmaking, or even just shooting home videos, will be more likely to respond to these characters.

TORBEN GRODAL

Grodal (1997: 93) describes identification as sharing the emotions of the characters and simulating the emotions. He suggests that cognitive identification does not have to lead to empathy but that it is likely to be a consequence of prolonged identification. The longer that we spend identifying with the characters (by being positioned in alignment with their point of view, for example) then the more likely it is that we will empathise with them by the end of the film. This would suggest why The Blair Witch Project has such a strong impact by the final scene when the audience is still trapped in the perspective of Heather as she runs around the mysterious house in the woods.

It is clear that there is a certain amount of agreement between these theorists but also room to further explore some of the ideas that surround identification and in particular regarding the aesthetics of The Blair Witch Project.

IDENTIFICATION WITH VICTIMS

Firstly, *The Blair Witch Project* differs from many of its horror film predecessors, particularly those in the slasher film sub-genre. If we are to assume that at least a small part of the filmmakers' technique of encouraging identification is by positioning the viewers in alignment with the point of view of the characters, then *The Blair Witch Project* is notable for making us identify with victims throughout.

In slasher films such as *Halloween* and *Friday the 13th* (1980), we are infamously encouraged to identify with the villains not the victims for much of the running time. *Halloween* opens with a long point of view shot that ends with the stabbing of a naked young woman in her bedroom. Only after this shocking scene is the audience allowed the reverse shot where we see whose point of view we have been sharing. Prior to the murder, the audience is taken on a first person subjective ride round a house as the character stalks and spies, watching a couple getting cosy on a sofa before going upstairs to have sex. The positioning of the spectator in the eyes of this voyeur makes us want to see more.

Similarly, when the director of *Friday the 13th* and its sequels wishes to suggest that Jason Vorhees (or his mother) is lurking nearby, a point of view shot is used. This point of view watches from the shadows as unsuspecting victims dance, party and have sex without any knowledge of their secret watcher. Slasher films like this fail to provide quite the same level of intense realism and fear in audiences. If the killer is like a reactionary father figure coming to strike at the wayward youth, the audience is positioned to identify and even cheer on the murderer who punishes their contemporaries on screen.

This is not the case with *The Blair Witch Project* where the traditionally young male audience of horror films is forced into identification mainly with a young woman and the monster is never seen nor even hinted at by subjective shots lurking in the woods. Even to the most misogynistic of young male viewers, it would be a very strange reaction to cheer on the witch as Heather becomes more and more distressed.

SUBJECTIVE AND POINT OF VIEW CAMERA

The Blair Witch Project also differs from these older examples of horror films with subjective camerawork in that it features a diegetic camera. In traditional point of view shots, the camera may be positioned where a character is within the diegesis but there is no actual camera in the world of the film, acknowledged by the characters or actually recording anything. On the other hand, the diegetic camera in *The Blair Witch Project* is more than a simple point of view shot. The camera is there in Heather's hands and the other characters can see it, discuss it and are using it to record their fates.

The diegetic camera is therefore subjective as the audience only sees what the character sees, but it is also different to the typical point of view shot in narrative cinema. This subjectivity traps the audience into the viewpoint of Heather with no escape. Myrick claimed they wanted 'to do something with long takes where the audience is stuck with the protagonists of the film - where the editing and the way the film is shot don't let you escape from the reality of what's going on with the characters' (Gallagher, 1999: 73). There are no objective shots to distance the viewer from the characters or to help them see the events from a neutral, omniscient perspective. *The Blair Witch Project* is unrelenting in forcing a perceptual identification with the characters holding the cameras. A film like this that limits all camera shots to a subjective perspective is very limited in where the camera can be placed. The camera can only be positioned where either a character can be or where they could put the camera themselves. Therefore, there can be no aerial shots showing how far from civilisation the characters are, no establishing shots that show the three characters sitting round a campfire at night and no shots of the parents, police or other potential characters worrying about the missing students. The audience is completely restricted to the experience of the victims. *The Blair Witch Project* may not be able to have the emotional punch of seeing Heather's Mum crying for her missing daughter but audiences will be more likely to feel Heather's fear if they are never given a break from it.

While video cameras are devices that enable a person to capture the real by seemingly only pointing and shooting, they also have limits. There are confines to what can be captured within the frame and therefore there are always restrictions on what can be seen. Cameras do not provide the full truth of any situation. In *The Blair Witch Project*, identification is enforced because both the viewer and the characters never see the monster. This witch that torments the students is never glimpsed on camera, never captured and contained and like Heather, Mike and Josh, we never see her. Because the witch remains forever out of shot, the audience is encouraged to feel the same anxiety, frustration and fear as the students who seek her. The endless point of view shots create between the viewer and the character what Smith (1995: 163) calls an 'identical limitation of knowledge, by what is withheld rather than what is given'.

Though we are perceptually identified with Heather for most of the film, a person watching it may not necessarily imagine her every thought or desire. However, we can often hear what she is thinking and how she is feeling. In her behind-the-scenes informal footage, she is frequently talking as she operates the camera. Though Heather may not be on screen when she is holding the camera and pointing it at Mike and Josh, we can still hear her contributions to conversations, her screams and her crying. The effect of these audible reactions can be as potent as the more traditional technique of using a close up to convey the emotions of a character. When Heather runs out of her tent into the darkness of the night, it is her screams from off camera that are most important in creating identification. Though the screen may be black, the spectator knows exactly what is going on in the character's head if not what is happening right in front of them. Hearing her screams but not seeing her face is like hearing our own screams while not being able to see our own face.

Similarly the movement and angles of the camera can reveal a great deal about the emotions of the user. Though many argue that the point of view shot has only limited options, there are a range of techniques that can be used to convey how the operator is feeling. Dropping the camera implies a lack of control, shakiness suggests uncertainty and fear, quick pans or tilts can reveal fright or edginess and zooms demonstrates an interest in an object. The overall sense of a lack of control and losing a grip on both the project and their sanity is revealed through the disintegration of the camerawork from the early scenes to the final shots. Whereas early in The Blair Witch Project, there is still some sense of structure and of setting the camera up carefully to document what is needed, the audience later gets the strong sense that this is the camerawork of three terrified young amateurs, completely unable to capture anything carefully.

What is most interesting about The Blair Witch Project's use of the point of view shot is that it lacks the traditional point of view structure that Smith (1995: 156) refers to.

Usually a point of view shot is signalled to the audience by a structured series of shots that help the viewer to read the shot as point of view. A close up of a character staring at something off camera is generally followed by a shot that shows the object that the person in the close up was looking at and then there is a cut back to the person still looking towards the object in the final shot of the sequence. However *The Blair Witch Project* lacks these shots of the characters' faces that surround the point of view shot. This point of view structure is not needed in the film as it is all shot from the perspective of the characters and no signalling to the viewer is needed when a point of view shot occurs. It could be argued that by not having the close ups, the audience lacks the opportunity of reading the performance of the actors and therefore identification will be decreased. However, the constant perceptual identification, along with the audible camera operators adds to the recognition of Heather's character and alignment that the spectator feels with her, if not the total allegiance with her actions.

Barry Keith Grant (2013) goes as far as to suggest that in films like *The Blair Witch Project*, the spectator's identification is actually aligned more with the camera than the character. Often a scene is presented from the point of view of only the camera and not a character. For example the infamous apology scene where Heather films herself in a very tight and slightly mis-framed close up is shot from where the camera is in her hand but not where her eyes are (as they are clearly on screen). The audience is unlikely to feel any sense of identification with the camera here despite sharing its position but the close up and opportunity to read Heather's face for emotional cues instead adds to the identification with her.

There are also attacks on the camera that make the audience feel threatened. When the film ends, it is the camera that falls to the floor and we actually have no idea what happens to Heather. It is the assault on the camera that registers and terrifies the audience, and thoughts of what happened to the character are intrinsically tied to the camera. Like in a first person shooter videogame, the spectator lives in the diegetic world through the camera rather than a character. In *The Blair Witch Project*, there are two cameras and the spectator lives through both, tied to not one but three characters, Mostly, it is Josh and Heather who film, but when Josh disappears, it is Heather and Mike who film the final scene.

The camera hits the floor but continues to film for a few moments.

CLOSE UPS

The importance of close ups, in order to maintain identification, is also often argued to be essential. How can the audience identify with someone they rarely see? Gaut (1999: 210) has argued that the reaction shot is far more effective at making a viewer empathise with a character than a point of view shot. He suggests the importance of seeing and reading the human face is more important than seeing from the point of view of a character. Witnessing the distress on Heather's face as she turns the camera on herself is more powerful than all the point of view shots in the rest of the film, according to this theory.

Audiences are experts in reading the human face for signs of emotion and a close up on a character, filling the frame with an excellent performance will likely create great sympathy and empathy for the character. It is interesting that Myrick and Sánchez chose to have Heather turn the camera around and film her own face on the final night in the tent. Poorly framed and lit, the shot itself reveals much about how Heather is feeling but it is the close up on the upper half of her face and particularly her bloodshot eyes and trembling voice that provide a great deal of the emotion and encourage viewers to empathise with her as the film approaches its climax.

Despite the vast importance of the point of view shots throughout *The Blair Witch Project*, a huge part of the identification with Heather is finally caused by her filming her own face in close up. The communication of emotions through this camera shot is as integral to this film as it was to the early films of the likes of D.W. Griffith back in the early 20th century. The fact that Heather Donahue is not a Hollywood star, but an ordinary looking girl who audiences were not familiar with before seeing the film, only adds to the identification of spectators. While point of view shots are important, identification is also promoted through the words she speaks, the chance to see the fear in her face and construction and recognition of her as a relatable character.

In conclusion, *The Blair Witch Project* should seemingly promote increased identification because viewers will empathise and sympathise more with characters if they continually see events restricted by their point of view. However, it has been argued that the lack of close ups, and opportunities for reading a character's expressions, can also have a distancing effect. At the same time, hearing the voice and screams of a character from behind the camera can also aid identification, almost as if the character's inner thoughts and vocalisation of these thoughts are injected into the viewer's head. We can imagine how Heather feels because of the way she holds the camera, what she films and how she films it. When turning the camera on herself, we get the much desired chance to see her distress and *The Blair Witch Project* becomes even more personal, and the character's hopelessness is even more unbearable. We are forced to identify with these students through the aesthetics of the film and the restriction to their experience of events, but identification emerges not as the product of any single technique. *The Blair Witch Project* is relentless in making us suffer along with Heather, Mike and Josh. There is no relief from hearing their thoughts, seeing what they see and sharing their experience of the horror.

REFERENCES

Balasz, B. (1945) 'Filming Death' In: Macdonald, K. And Cousins M. (eds) *Imagining reality*. London: Faber and Faber

Carroll, N. (1990) *The Philosophy of Horror or Paradoxes of the Heart*. London: Routledge.

Gallagher, S. (1999) 'Into the Woods.' *Filmmaker.* 7 (2), 72-74.

Gaut, B. (1999) 'Identification and emotion in narrative film' In: Platinga, C. And Smith, G. (eds) *Passionate Views: film, cognition and emotion.* London: The John Hopkins University Press.

Grant, B. (2013) 'Digital anxiety and the new verité horror and sf film.' *Science Fiction Film and Television.* 6 (2), 153-175.

Grodal, T. (1997) *Moving Pictures: a new theory of film genres, feelings, and cognition.* Oxford: Clarendon Press.

Metz, C. (1982) *The Imaginary Signifier: Psychoanalysis and the Cinema.* Bllomington: Indiana University Press

Neill, A. (1996) 'Empathy and (film) fiction' In: Bordwell, D. and Carroll, N. (eds) *Post-theory: reconstructing film studies.* London: The University of Wisconsin Press.

Packham, C. (2012) 'The Rise of Found-Footage Horror.' Available: http://www.villagevoice.com/2012-10-17/film/the-rise-of-found-footage-horror-paranormal-activity-4/. [Accessed 23 September 2013].

Smith, M. (1995) *Engaging Characters: fiction, emotion and the cinema.* Oxford: Clarendon Press.

4. FEAR OF THE DARK: WITCHES, WOMEN AND THE WOODS

Horror texts are often indicative of audience's particular fears and anxieties and reflect the times they are made. The American horror films of the 1970s were notable for bringing their horror home to the doorsteps of American families. They reflected the assassinations happening on home soil and the war raging in Vietnam that had tainted the American psyche. Benjamin Poole (2012) argued convincingly that *Saw* (2004) and to a lesser extent its sequels were products of post-9/11 fear and anxieties. So where does *The Blair Witch Project* sit and what late 90s fears does it represent in its story of kids lost in the woods and at the mercy of a malevolent witch?

The Blair Witch Project must be read as an old-fashioned but timeless ghost story in many ways. It is about people hunting for proof of the supernatural and at the same time being terrorised by something far beyond their understanding. The film purports to be an eyewitness account of something terrifying and never truly and indisputably captured by film or photography. However, no supernatural occurrences are concretely confirmed and instead what it documents is mysterious rock piles and stick men hung in trees that are symbolic and suggestive of the menace lurking in the woods. It is a film that plays on audience desire to see indisputable proof of the supernatural while also withholding that irrefutable evidence.

There are clearly some deeply held fears that have been found in societies since storytelling began that are being recycled in *The Blair Witch Project*. But equally this film is taking the witches and lost in the woods familiarity of fairytales like Hansel and Gretel and replaying them in a new and very modern way. Hansel and Gretel now have cameras to record what happens to them, their breadcrumbs are a useless map and compass and their witch's house is no longer made of sweets but decaying walls covered in the hand prints of children. The youths of the film are a generation shaped by technology, dependant on it and ultimately failed by it. The camera, and particularly Heather's dependence on it, brings about their downfall.

THE CAMERA AND THE FAILURE OF TECHNOLOGY

Heather cannot hide behind the camera forever, and soon enough the tables are turned.

It is important to take *The Blair Witch Project*'s most distinctive aspect and consider it in terms of the fear it causes in both the characters and the audience. The camera is a central prop in the film. While it may not be that often shown on screen (except when two cameras are rolling at the same time and one films the other), the audience is constantly aware of the presence of the camera due to the dialogue, operator's off screen voice and shaky framing. Some have argued that the fundamental theme of *The Blair Witch Project* is the failure of technology and what makes the film so scary is the complete loss of control that the characters experience.

The camera is present in the diegesis because the characters want to document the history of the Blair Witch legend. Their task is to create a documentary for part of their filmmaking course. They are naïve students; young and relatively innocent compared to the sexualised, drink- and drug-taking teens of many slasher films. The camera is a means of control and they use it to try to render the supernatural less scary. By exploring the roots of the Blair Witch, they seek to explain and to reveal the mystery behind the myth. It is clear that Heather does not take the stories that seriously when she is questioning the people of the town. All of the three filmmakers find Mary Brown, who claims to have seen the witch, to be a bit loopy and they suspect she is a liar.

The camera serves many functions in the film. As the narrative progresses, it becomes less about capturing footage for a documentary and more a tool for Heather to hide behind. Mike attacks her constant filming and then turns the camera on to her. He accuses her of using the camera as a barrier between her and reality, saying 'It's not the same on film is it? I mean, you know it's real, but it's like looking through the lens gives you some sort of protection from what's on the other side.' Josh similarly maintains 'It's not quite reality. It's like a totally filtered reality. It's like you can pretend everything's not quite the way it is.' Just as Heather is not safe from the witch just because she is looking through the lens of a camera, the film attempts to imply that the audience is not safe because they are looking through a screen. *The Blair Witch Project* breaks down the barriers between fact and fiction. It makes viewers feel the same sense of fear that children might feel at scary films; the sense that what they are watching could in fact be real.

Heather uses the camera as a defence against what is happening; it gives her a sense of security while also distancing her from the others in the group. Heather feels increasingly threatened as the project continues to unravel and perhaps partly due to her gender, feels she needs extra protection from her two male companions. Though Mike and Josh are never truly threatening towards Heather, tempers do rise and Heather becomes the target of their anger for a number of reasons. Heather started out as the controlling director of the project, confident and assertive, but as the film goes on she becomes less and less sure of herself, as do her crew. The lack of control is reflected in the increasingly erratic cinematography but is also clear from Donohue's performance and dialogue. The camera captures less and less useful footage for the student film and more and more of the disintegration of the group and the mental health and stability of the individuals.

Bryan Alexander (2004) argues that *The Blair Witch Project* is all about the student filmmakers' expulsion from adulthood. The film begins with Heather in her home, preparing for a journey away from the comforts of civilisation with a pair of young men. It is an opportunity for freedom and for the trio to prove themselves as capable adults and semi-professional filmmakers, all of which they fail at. Instead, what is documented by the cameras is their reversion to childhood. Heather, Mike and Josh might drink a bit of alcohol, sleep in the same tents and begin their project successfully but they soon lose all control and sense of independence. Their cynicism and semi-professional manner becomes bickering, screaming, swearing and crying. They yearn for the comfort of their homes and civilisation and Heather eventually cries for and apologises for her earlier trepidation. Notably she asks for forgiveness from parents showing her complete regression to a childlike state; emotional, terrified and desperate for adults to step in and save her. Alexander also notes that it then becomes the responsibility of the police and whoever edits the footage to finish the failed documentary. The youngsters go out into the world very sure of themselves but cannot survive on their own. They cannot even complete the task of making a documentary and it is left to adults to find the footage and piece together what happened to them.

The natural world and, it is insinuated, the supernatural world beat Heather, Mike and Josh; defeating them, withholding its mysteries and making them wish they were back in the arms of their parents safe at home. Even the camera cannot capture the full horror of what happened to them or provide any exact and precise proof of the fate of the filmmakers. Similarly, both the map and the compass are technologies that fail them when they are most needed. Even with these tools for steering them safely home, they get lost in the woods. Mike throws away the map in a tantrum and the compass is either broken or the witch's power extends to being able to manipulate it. Either way, Heather and her small crew become hopelessly lost in the woods despite Heather's protests that America doesn't have enough woods left to get lost in, exclaiming 'This is America! We've exhausted all of our natural resources!'

This is typical of Heather's assuredness and also her naivety. Similarly her determination to keep filming also results in disaster when it comes to the end of the film. Her stubborn refusal to stop filming and to keep investigating, as well as Mike's own gung-ho approach, lead to the pair entering a house with very little sense of their own safety.

Their determination to capture proof of the supernatural or to capture evidence of what is happening to them clouds their judgement. Video evidence would be indisputable if only it captured some sign that the witch was truly real. Like a good ghost story can only be told by someone who believes they witnessed the presence of a ghost, *The Blair Witch Project* could be a great witch hunt story if only its young filmmakers managed to capture the witch on camera. The desire to capture proof also makes the filmmakers childlike as they seek something to convince them they are not liars or fakers. Even when they are in grave danger, like those war reporters that came before them or ghost hunters on reality television shows, they aim for technological evidence to document what they experienced.

However, by withholding this indisputable proof of the existence of the witch, *The Blair Witch Project* is potentially far scarier for the audience. By tapping into childhood fears of the dark and unknown, both the characters and the audience are kept fearing the worst that their imagination can come up with.

WITCHES

Witches have often been used as the scary villain in classic stories from *Macbeth* to *The Wizard of Oz* (1939) to *The Blair Witch Project* and the recent *The Lords of Salem* (2012) and beyond. The representation of women as witches has often been criticised as a reactionary stereotype of strange women, intelligent women, healers and ugly or red haired women. Witches are inextricably tied in with representations of women who are different and refuse to be bound by social and restrictive gender norms.

As far back as the silent era of cinema, the mock-documentary format was used to convince the audiences that what they were witnessing was 'real life' caught on camera. *Häxan: Witchcraft Through the Ages* (1922) offers a historical overview of witchcraft and is a documentary that appears educational in intent by showing a slideshow of images but then becomes increasingly less 'real' as a series of re-enactments of witches and devil worshipping are included in the film. The mix of traditional *mise-en-scène* elements of the horror film such as witches and devils along with actors and sets being used in the documentary format is a clear forebear to *The Blair Witch Project*.

The idea of witchcraft emerged from the early practices of healing women who used homeopathic treatments to cure people with illnesses back in the days before modern medicine was available. Women who had knowledge of homemade remedies and natural medicine would often be midwives and were called upon to assist in any instances where pain relief was required. With the spread of Christianity came repressive practices, and attitudes towards healers turned sour. 'Men of God' would accuse healers of being anti-God or even devil worshippers, arguing that only they could heal people and that some illnesses were punishment from God for sins committed by the person. Wise women with healing powers became feared and outcast, accused of ungodly sorcery, pagan practices and black magic.

The clergy did not like the power of these wise women and representations of witches as ugly, destructive hags became common and people turned against them as they embraced Christianity. Witches embodied evil in the eyes of the church and though many healers went underground, the Christian church brewed hysteria in the masses until they felt the need to hunt down these once treasured and respected women. The phrase 'witch hunt' is still often used when people get hysterically stirred up (often by the media) into a state of moral panic in society, whether it be Communists in the 1950s or paedophiles or Muslim extremists in recent years.

Women accused of witchcraft were tried quickly and often in ridiculous ways and hung or burnt alive in public to scare the community into conformity and obedience of the Christian church. Allegations were hurled at countless women and they were blamed for all sorts of unfortunate events. They were accused of casting spells and cursing communities and no woman was safe from the eyes of the Church and the brainwashed congregation. Women who did not regularly attend church or were poor or homeless were most at risk due to their poor standing in the eyes of the community.

The Blair Witch Project timeline of events that lead up to the disappearance of the three student filmmakers uses this history of witches and fails to challenge the stereotype of witchcraft and witches as evil forces. The witch Elly Keward is cast out after trying to snatch children and then when she supposedly dies in the woods, her spirit remains to haunt the area and continues to attack children and adults alike. Elly Kedward goes from evil woman to supernatural force that cannot be stopped. She is destructive, all powerful and even able to manipulate the hermit Rustin Parr to do her dastardly deeds for her. There is no suggestion that Kedward was ever a wise, healing lady, wrongly accused by the townsfolk. She was evil as a human and worse as a ghost. Her powers beyond death no doubt come from some unnatural union with the devil or some other witchcraft that allows her to deny death. Though she is never seen in the film, her history and the suggestions of her power make her a very stereotypical and reactionary version of an evil witch.

REPRESENTATION OF WOMEN

The Blair Witch Project could be considered misogynist in its use of a female villain but also because the central character Heather is a strong female who is eventually broken down and crushed by her own failure. While it can be argued that Heather begins as a positive and progressive representation of a young woman, she eventually becomes a weak, quivering, screaming victim; a Final Girl with no fight left in her and unable to defeat the villain. Though *The Blair Witch Project* is interesting for its lack of sexualising the subject, it still has a female that fails to achieve her goal or keep herself and her crew safe. She starts empowered and ends the film useless. While the male gaze is never an issue with Heather as much of the film is filmed from her perspective and the issue of gender and sexual attraction or behaviour is never a major concern of the film, she is still the one responsible for the deaths of her crew. Her stereotypically masculine traits such as being head strong and proud make her foolish and culpable, not heroic. By the end of the film, she is convinced that everything that has happened is all her fault and she is apologetic, defeated and, some might argue, punished for trying to dominate her male peers.

What is notably missing from *The Blair Witch Project* is any physical representation of Elly Kedward, the witch that is supposed to haunt the woods around Burkittsville. None of the familiar tropes of what a witch looks like are even referenced in *The Blair Witch Project*. There are no black cats, no brooms or flying old hags, no cauldron and no hook-nosed old crone wandering the woods dressed all in black. Elly Kedward evades being recorded by the cameras of the filmmakers and lives only in the imagination of the viewer and the students. Though some of the locals claim to have seen her in the form of a mist rising out of water and a hairy armed half beast, these sightings are never confirmed and could simply be the product of over active childlike imaginations. Though Elly Kedward was definitely a woman, the film never dwells on the gender of the entity now haunting the woods.

The mythology that surrounds the film deals with Elly Kedward in greater depth but is not fully developed within the film and instead was only revealed in ancillary sources such as the internet site http://www.blairwitch.com/ and the accompanying fake documentary, *The Curse of the Blair Witch*. Elly Kedward was a woman accused of luring children into her home in order to try and extract their blood. She was tried and banished to the woods outside the town in a harsh winter and left to die. Forty years later in 1825, eleven witnesses see a pale woman's hand emerge from a creek to pull in a ten-year-old girl whose body is never recovered. Another sixty years later, an entire search party looking for a missing boy is found dead and disembowelled at Coffin Rock. Then in 1941, Rustin Parr an old hermit who lives in the woods admits to abducting and murdering seven children in his home which he says he did for an old woman ghost who lives in the woods nearby. While Kedward's guilt never appears to be questioned and her supernatural powers can only be assumed to have come from some sorcery, it is interesting that an old *man* is the physical representation of evil at the end of Elly Kedward's history.

Though Elly Kedward is never visible in *The Blair Witch Project*, she is certainly a presence that permeates much of the film. The signs that she is causing mischief and eventually murder are all present for viewers willing to take a leap of faith. The rock piles, the hanging stick men, the sound of cackling and children crying late in the night and finally the home of Rustin Parr and Mike standing in the corner of the room facing the wall all have her fingerprints on them. All signs point to a supernatural explanation for what happened to Heather, Mike and Josh; an explanation that is rendered more believable because the footage does not either confirm or deny it.

THE SUPERNATURAL

The Blair Witch Project is also a culturally significant document that suggests that people in the west still have fears surrounding the occult and the supernatural. The idea that some early viewers of the film believed it to be genuine footage reinforces the idea that audiences are not as secular as is often suggested. The film plays on particular fears from childhood; the frightening woods, being lost, alone, unable to see in the dark, and, of course, witches. The characters revert quickly to childhood when faced with such fears in the film because there is something primal about them.

According to one survey, '45 percent of Americans still believe in ghosts, or that the spirits of dead people can come back in certain places and situations' (Speigel, 2013).

Organised religion in the west may be in decline, but a belief, and even more so, a fear, of the supernatural is still surprisingly prevalent.

What makes the fear of the supernatural in *The Blair Witch Project* so profound is that its representation can scare both sceptics and believers alike. By not revealing any ghostly apparitions, it is impossible to argue with the verisimilitude of events depicted. Something is definitely taunting Heather, Mike and Josh and by keeping itself completely unseen, it makes the events impossible to dismiss as unrealistic or clearly fake. An easier answer would be that some locals are just playing games with the trio and this is what Mike suggests is happening at first. Nothing that happens in the film has to be considered supernatural but by the end, the complete lack of appearance of anything either supernatural or otherwise to explain the events, causes the audience to fear the worst. The surrounding mythology of course also allows the audience and even Heather, Mike and Josh to make an educated guess as to what is happening to them.

THE DARK

One of mankind's most basic and primal fears is of the dark. As is stated in the special features of *The Blair Witch Project* DVD, 'fear in evolutionary terms is self-preservation'. Our ancestors were afraid of the dark because this is when they were at their weakest and most vulnerable. Human beings do not see well in the dark like some other creatures and this makes them more defenceless if they are attacked at night or in a dark place. This makes our fear of darkness innate and instinctive despite the fact we have less to fear from predators in the modern world.

The Blair Witch Project plays on that instinctive fear of the dark. The directing methods of Myrick and Sánchez would also emphasise the genuine fear of the actors at the time of shooting. Heather, Mike and Josh (the actors and the characters) are alone in the woods. This location is a generally dark place even during the day. The trees hide the light and things only get worse when night falls. Camping in the woods over night can be terrifying at the best of times with strange noises audible and the all encompassing darkness only broken by torches or candles. Sleeping in the wild is not a common occurrence for most contemporary people in the west and the sounds of the

Pitch black:
Heather runs for
her life at night.

wilderness will be particularly strange, alarming and unnerving to those used to the modern comforts of a bedroom in a house.

The characters in *The Blair Witch Project* cannot see much beyond their own lights. Their frequent cries of 'what is that?' show that they are listening hard for clues as to what is bothering them in the night but they are unable to see. Without light, they have to rely on the rest of their senses. Humans depend on sight beyond all other senses and to have this taken away in a strange place is a terrifying prospect. The scenes set at night are the scariest and will strike a chord with most audiences who recognise the instinctive desire to be able to see in order to survive a night alone in the woods.

When fear takes hold of a subject, the heart rate can increase greatly, they can hyperventilate, forcing more oxygen into their lungs, their pupils can dilate heightening their visual sense and their body becomes primed for escape or confrontation. *The Blair Witch Project* shows these biological consequences of fear on the human body. The sound of the characters' breathing is constantly heard in times of stress and their first instinct is often to run when they feel threatened. In the final frames of the film, Heather is both running and hyperventilating as she meets her fate in the dark house.

GUILT

The most infamous scene of *The Blair Witch Project* is where Heather decides to turn the camera on herself and apologise to all those that she feels she has let down. This is a clear manifestation of Heather's guilt at how events have transpired. Survivors of horrific ordeals often experience guilt because they have survived while others have not been so fortunate. Heather has already lost Josh and is at this point terrified she is either losing her mind or about to lose her own life. Her fear is palpable and she clearly feels responsible for what has happened. She lists the reasons this is so and apologises to her family and her crew.

Heather is unable to see that whatever is happening to them is not strictly her fault. She is not attacking or frightening or harming anybody and there are external (and likely supernatural) forces that are beyond her control. Things could have been done differently but Heather is not thinking clearly due to her fear, hunger and fatigue. Her guilt at Josh's disappearance is making her suffer even more than her own paralysing fear of the darkness. Those who experience guilt are punishing themselves. If they suffer enough, they believe, perhaps they can hope to earn forgiveness. Heather clearly suffers but it is too late to earn anyone's forgiveness by this point in the film.

SLEEP DEPRIVATION, COLD AND HUNGER

In order to feel safe, humans must feel their basic needs are being met. Food, shelter and sleep are vital physiological needs that must be met in order for a person to be able to function properly psychologically. If someone is sleep deprived, cold and hungry, their responses will slow down and their ability to survive in a dangerous situation may decrease. Without food and sleep, confusion, disorientation, paranoia and even hallucination can occur.

Again *The Blair Witch Project* deliberately plays on the fears of the actors, characters and the audience by making the situation as frightening as it can possibly be. The actors were given less and less food to survive on as the shoot progressed. They really slept in the woods at night and experienced the cold and hunger. The production team also kept them walking long distances during the day and kept them awake at night by scaring them. The performances of the actors easily reflect the states of mind of the characters. Both actors and characters are exhausted, hungry and cold. Lost in the woods and confused and disorientated, it is easy for the audience to identify with their predicament.

Their chances of survival drastically drop due to their mental and physical states. Even before the map is lost, they are confused by the appearance of the woods, disorientated by the compass and not working together as a group. They have packed too much equipment and it is tiring them out more than if they had travelled lighter. Heather has it the worst as team leader. She does not have the trust or respect of her crew. Mike and Josh are continually bickering with her and they fail to work as a team and look after each other when the going gets tough. What is worse than being stuck in the woods in a small group? Being stuck in the woods when your team cannot function properly and you would probably be better off alone. They scream at each other and physically fight at one point. Due in part to their lack of sleep and food, they are at each other's throats and no help to each other. Hell, it seems, really is other people.

REFERENCES

Alexander, B. (2004) 'The Blair Witch Project: expulsion from adulthood and versions of the American Gothic' In: Higley, S. L. and J. A. Weinstock (eds) (2004) *Nothing That Is: Millennial Cinema and the Blair Witch Controversies*. Detroit: Wayne State University Press

Laycock, J. (2011) 'What If It's Real?: Live-record Horror and Popular Belief in the Supernatural.' OI3Media Available from: http://host.uniroma3.it/riviste/OI3Media/Laycock. html

Poole, B. (2012) *Saw (Devil's Advocates)*. Leighton Buzzard: Auteur. 61-75

Speigel, L. (2013) 'Spooky Number of Americans Believe in Ghosts.' *The Huffington Post*. http://www.huffingtonpost.com/2013/02/02/real-ghosts-americans-poll_n_2049485.html

The Blair Witch Project DVD Special Features

5. MARKETING, RECEPTION AND LEGACY

This chapter will give an overview of how *The Blair Witch Project* was marketed, how it was received by critics and audiences and the legacy that endures more than a decade after its release. The distributors of *The Blair Witch Project* used ancillary media methods including a detailed website that immersed the browser in the mythology of the film and an accompanying documentary, *The Curse of the Blair Witch*. After the Sundance screening that allowed the filmmakers to sell it to distributor Artisan, the marketing became a huge part of making *The Blair Witch Project* the phenomenon it was in 1999. It affected the reception with audiences being encouraged to see the film as just one more part of a larger experience and helped build the legacy that would make *The Blair Witch Project* such an enduring part of popular culture with spoofs, a sequel, porn versions and a whole sub-genre of horror imitating it by copying the found footage format.

Since the mid-90s, the internet has become a huge tool for communication with more and more internet users across the globe each year. Its impact on commerce and culture is widespread and *The Blair Witch Project* was one of the first films to fully explore the potential of the internet as a marketing tool. The internet was fast becoming a medium of discovery meaning that fans of the film had to explore and find their way around the web to find out more about the Blair Witch mythology and this augmented the sense of authenticity surrounding the film at the time of release. It also made many spectators an active part of the marketing as they sought it out for themselves rather than having it forced upon them.

The rise of the internet could even be conceived as having had an impact on the story and shooting style of the film. Cherry (2009: 187) argued of *The Blair Witch Project* that 'the unremitting point of view camerawork predates and anticipates the documentation of everyday life now in evidence on blogs, YouTube, webcams and other internet sites'. Not only is it the restriction to one person's point of view but it is also the capturing of the seemingly mundane; the arguments, the boredom and the tedium of being lost in the woods. Video bloggers and those with webcams can film themselves endlessly talking about anything they wish to and then upload it for all to see on the internet.

The Blair Witch Project descends from student documentary to the arguing of a group of scared and lost kids and then finally to news-worthy footage of the final moments before the disappearance of these young adults. It is the sort of footage that could easily be uploaded to the internet in the age of digital cameras and people promoting their own daily lives as entertainment.

MARKETING

However the impact of the internet was most crucial to the success of *The Blair Witch Project* due to the website that was used to market the film. Films have had promotional websites associated with them since *Stargate* (1994) but the web was still a medium in relative infancy in the 1990s compared to what it is today and *The Blair Witch Project's* use of the internet was considered revolutionary by many. Speaking in 2013, actor Michael C. Williams explained what he considers to be the reason for the film's success:

> In 1998 we were all figuring out maybe two years into this whole world wide web, basically what you read, you believed... at that point home video cameras were really more accessible for the first time. They weren't these huge things. So to me a perfect storm of where the internet was at its infancy and home video cameras... you could relate to us because it was the first time that you were seeing something on the big screen that you would usually watch on your TV.'

The interactive nature of the marketing meant that a large audience had found the film even before its release and due to the nature of the open ending and only small hints at the mythology within the film, audiences were also likely to return to the website after viewing the film. The website (www.blairwitch.com) detailed the mythology behind the Blair Witch and presented the three student stars of the film as 'The Filmmakers'. It completely destabilised audience perceptions of the film as either real or fake, never giving away if the film was 'real' or not.

Viral marketing is common now with film studios attempting to create a buzz around their film by getting the audience to spread the word on the film through social media and the internet. *Cloverfield* (2008), *The Dark Knight* (2008) and *Prometheus* (2012) have all created websites that extend the universes created in the films and give fans something to engage with beyond the cinema experience. *The Blair Witch Project* nurtured fan cultures from the start with a website that sparked endless debate over the veracity of the events depicted. Curious people would investigate beyond the official website and engage in heated discussion on forums where the authenticity of the film would be questioned and interrogated by eager fans; the very definition of active spectators. Their dissemination of material about the film caused word of mouth to spread and *The Blair Witch Project* became a movie that needed to be discovered by people. People interacted around it and the mythology and carefully created website augmented its hold on people's imaginations.

The website became a hub for a community of fans who would communicate with each other and share their knowledge of the film with others. It became more than simply an advertising tool and as with all good viral marketing, spread naturally and aggressively across the internet and into popular culture. In creating what looked like a true story through its aesthetics and ancillary media, *The Blair Witch Project* brewed speculation and manufactured doubt in the minds of many. The website became just another part of what Telotte (2004: 38) calls 'a complex web of information sites'. It framed the narrative of the film, providing context, depth, back story and further 'proof' of the 'truth' of the film. Viewers of the film are encouraged by the lack of answers and the realistic construction to go beyond the cinema or home viewing experience and to investigate the story further.

This makes *The Blair Witch Project* stand out from its contemporaries as a different and relatively new form of entertainment and spectacle. Rather than just being perceived as a stand alone traditional fiction horror film, the promotional website and the form of the film itself positions it as a piece of documentary evidence; a literal piece of found footage that was discovered and screened for audiences. The website adds to this footage by showing 'evidence' that complements it. There are police photos of Josh's car, the tape and the film reel and the bag they were found in, photos of the search for the students and frame grabs of the news reports that covered the disappearance. The film itself is just one more artefact in this tapestry of deception.

The use of the internet is particularly pertinent as it is the unrestricted medium where people are well aware that they can find virtually anything. *The Blair Witch Project* may find its way on to cinema screens and on to home entertainment formats and therefore reveal itself to be a product of the media industry but the website and the materials gathered and displayed on it suggest that there is more to the film than mere fiction. The internet is the place where millions of voices can be heard and access cannot be restricted. The website offers more knowledge to those keen to find out the truth behind the movie but like the internet in general only manages to cloud the truth and make it more inaccessible.

Fandom has found a happy home on the internet with fans of genres, stars or individual films communicating and sharing a sense of camaraderie over their common love of movies. Fans have always felt the impulse to praise and critique work that is of interest to them, but fandom is a more modern phenomenon. There are now organised communities of fans, some of which have their own commonly used names such as Whovians, Trekkies and Twihards. The history of fandom highlights the importance of science fiction as a genre that inspired fans to begin meeting and engaging in fan-related activities. However, horror fanzines emerged out of science fiction fandom in the 1960s and 70s and since then, horror conventions, film festivals and websites have become increasingly important parts of contemporary fandom. The move from print fanzines to internet fandom was occurring in the years that *The Blair Witch Project* first made its appearance, complete with fan-baiting website.

During the 1990s, many fans were beginning to get involved in online fan activities such as joining mailing lists and starting to host their own fan sites. Fanfiction archives began to be made publicly available and so fans had easy access to things they would have previously had to meet other fans in person for. Also, those dedicated enough to be writing their own fanfiction were soon able to upload their own contributions to websites with little to no knowledge of coding. Sites like FanFiction.net and LiveJournal pre-empted the social media of today by adding the ability to have friends lists and leave comments, therefore encouraging continuing community interaction.

Horror fans have always been particularly notable for their obsessive fan activities and the internet helps them to share their passion (and hatred) with others. *The Blair Witch Project* therefore perfectly captured its target audience by giving horror fans more to talk about, discuss, debate and explore through the unconventional promotional website.

As Williams said, people were just getting their heads around the internet in 1999 when the film was released. According to Internet World Stats, the number of people using the internet grew exponentially in the late 1990s from 16 million in 1995 to 304 million by March 2000. A Starburst Magazine article states that the *Blair Witch* website had over 20 million hits *before* the film was released, and then after it was released, started regularly receiving around two million hits every day.

However the marketing and ancillary media did not begin and end with the website. Another huge part of the marketing and myth-making of *The Blair Witch Project* was the mock-documentary *The Curse of the Blair Witch* screened on the Sci-fi channel two days before the actual film premiered in New York.

Using the footage that Myrick and Sánchez shot but decided to exclude from the final feature, it took the form of an expositional documentary, using all the codes and conventions to create a convincing mock-documentary. Utilising interviews with fake 'experts' and 'authentic' documents such as photos and new reports, *The Curse of the Blair Witch* offers more of the mythology and positions the film and website as further pieces of a bigger puzzle.

Actors are cast and interviewed as real people including Heather's film professor, her best friend and grandfather. Real photos of Heather as a child are used and documents including her thesis proposal are shown. Tom Williams (Mike's brother) plays himself and all the actors keep their actual first names in the documentary, further blurring the boundaries between fact and fiction. It uses clips from the actual film ('courtesy of Artisan Entertainment') and constructs a picture of the students before they left for the fateful trip to the woods. It is a wholly convincing documentary that seeks to establish the students as real people and the mythology of Elly Kedward becoming the Blair Witch as occasionally disputed but also frequently agreed and documented fact. A professor of folklore and a historian contribute to the documentary in interviews and their testimony often adds scepticism to the official version of events but then as the documentary continues, the evidence mounts up that something supernatural occurred in the woods.

What all these pieces of marketing do according to Schopp (2004: 137) is to compromise 'the "safety" of the experience' of watching the *The Blair Witch Project*.

Viewers with any doubts over the veracity of the events depicted in the film will get the 'full' experience by having their safety and perceived distance from fictional events destabilised. The legacy of the Blair Witch and the chronology of events leading up to the filmmakers' disappearance is all worked out and displayed for audiences who want to look beyond the film.

RECEPTION

The Blair Witch Project was the horror phenomenon of 1999 and arguably the entire 1990s, reviving the genre that had been in the doldrums since the endless slasher cycle of the 80s and only just on its way to a seriously self-referential revival with 1996's *Scream*. In a year that should have been dominated by *Star Wars: Episode I: The Phantom Menace*, *The Blair Witch Project* stole many headlines and became the most profitable horror film of all time (only recently overtaken by *Paranormal Activity*). Taking nearly $250 million at the box office off its tiny budget, *The Blair Witch Project* divided audiences and critics alike but many were quick to praise its efficiency and even to call it the 'new face of movie horror'.

Winning the Golden Raspberry Award (Razzie) for Worst Actress as well as the Independent Spirit John Cassavetes Award for Best Film, *The Blair Witch Project* made some experience motion sickness but was mostly critically acclaimed. With an 87% fresh rating on Rotten Tomatoes, but only 6.3 stars out of 10 from user reviews on the Internet Movie Database, it appears *The Blair Witch Project* was often a victim of ludicrously high expectations created by critics' reviews.

Peter Travers of Rolling Stone Magazine could see the potential of *The Blair Witch Project* to change the future of horror calling it 'a groundbreaker in fright that reinvents scary for the new millennium'. He also pointed to the lack of nudity and gore of so many past horrors and like many others mentions both George Lucas and Hitchcock in his review of the film. He praises the film for being made on a budget 'that couldn't buy George Lucas a proper car. It's what you don't see in *The Blair Witch Project* that pumps your adrenalin and, in the best Hitchcock tradition, keeps you hanging on.'

Unsurprisingly much of the ink spilled about the film paid particular attention to the visual style with David Denby from The New Yorker calling it a 'cunningly conceived and crafted exercise in suggestibility and terror.' Ann Hornaday from The Baltimore Sun gave credit to the directors saying 'most of the credit for how scarily effective The Blair Witch Project is goes to Myrick and Sánchez, who faithfully hew to the first principle of horror – never, ever show the monster.' Many mention the handheld camera work and rough aesthetics of the film but Slate's David Edelstein goes further in pinning down more specifically why The Blair Witch Project is so effective stating: 'They have reanimated the genre not by adding to it but subtracting from it.' He goes on to pin point the techniques used by the directors that have the most impact: 'The first thing they've done is remove the omniscient point of view... we see even less [than the characters], since we lack their peripheral vision... as she [Heather] throws a look into the trees and shrieks: "What is that? What the fuck is that?" We never see what the fuck that is. If we did, some part of us would probably relax, because it would look like a special effect. But no part of us is allowed to relax. Ever.'

Garth Franklin of Dark Horizons also draws attention to the difference between The Blair Witch Project and other horrors, noting that the film 'doesn't rely on sudden scares that make you jump but rather drawn out unnerving tension which starts at zero and finishes with one of the most abrupt and shocking endings that you'll remember for a long time to come.' He is one of only a few critics to highlight the power of the ending, as well as the mood that is created throughout the film.

Despite that Razzie win for Heather Donahue, many critics praised the film for its trio of central performances. Sight and Sound's Charles Taylor considered 'the unmediated hysteria we see the actors sliding into is part of what makes the film so terrifying. It's also what makes it so unpleasant.' The A.V. Club's Keith Phipps adds 'Its three principals (Heather Donahue, Michael C. Williams, and Joshua Leonard) all give fine performances, creating fully realized characters from apparently candid moments in the film's first half and doing a thoroughly convincing job of appearing scared witless in its second.' Ann Hornaday compares the unknown stars of The Blair Witch Project with Tom Cruise and Nicole Kidman in Stanley Kubrick's Eyes Wide Shut (1999) stating 'whereas features two huge stars and has all the emotional immediacy of a storefront window, The Blair Witch Project features a cast of unknowns and packs an emotional wallop entirely disproportionate to its meager pedigree.' Hornaday also touches here on another aspect that many critics missed; the emotional engagement that audiences find with particularly Heather by the end of the film.

Her review is in opposition to Charles Taylor's from Sight and Sound that argues 'by banishing psychology, characterisation and finally humanity from their film, by excluding anything but sensation, the effect is ultimately not that much different from that of, say, *Armageddon*.' He does however recognise that the film has its merits, favourably comparing it to George A. Romero's feature debut in a back-handed compliment: 'because the film is so deliberately lacking in 'art' in much the same way *Night of the Living Dead* (1968) was, you can be lulled into thinking what you're seeing is actually happening.' What Taylor seems to miss is the art in the artlessness in a similar way to how many critics say the film has no special effects when in a sense the whole film is a special effect.

In their review, Total Film went beyond the techniques used to create the aesthetics and noted that *The Blair Witch Project* 'excels in playing upon the most primal of human emotions: fear, hunger and the despairing realisation that you are lost and you are going to die – and there's nothing you can do to prevent it from happening'. The idea and content is highlighted, as well as the techniques used to create it.

User reviews on IMDb range from the hysterical to the nonplussed with some raving about the film and some wondering what all the fuss is about. One user, Blackheart, argues 'without the overpowering F/X and music score most movies rely on to "scare" you, if you still have an imagination left what is implied becomes a hundred times scarier than anything offered up by Hollywood in the last 30 years'. Most of the highly rated user reviews praise the film for forcing audiences to use their imagination and for playing up the fear of the unknown. On the other hand those that hated *The Blair Witch Project* call it boring, a waste of time and not engaging or scary. Matt from Texas' review is typical: 'I spent about an hour and a half sitting around in my living room on Halloween waiting for something...anything to happen. Just when I thought it was coming to the big climax at the end in the house, nothing happens.'

LEGACY

With all the surrounding mythology that Myrick and Sánchez created, there were many ways in which they could exploit it from books and comic books to soundtracks and sequels. Spin offs from the film included D.A. Stern's *The Blair Witch Project: A Dossier*. Like the website and *The Curse of the Blair Witch* documentary, it again presented the actual film as a factual document and the book contained more in the way of fabricated evidence to back up the mythology. Police reports, pictures, newspaper articles and transcriptions of interviews are collected together in the 'dossier' to elaborate on the missing filmmakers as well as the stories of Elly Kedward and Rustin Parr.

Stern later wrote two novels based around the mythology but with semi-original storylines. In 2000, *Blair Witch: The Secret Confession of Rustin Parr* was published, detailing the journal entries of the priest who heard serial killer Parr's last confession before he was hung for murdering the children of the town of Burkittsville. It is a short and chilling expansion of the mythology that leaves readers with clues and questions about what really happened in the basement between Parr and the only surviving child of his massacre, Kyle Brody. Then in 2004 Stern returned to the Blair Witch universe with another novel *Blair Witch: Graveyard Shift,* this time with entirely original characters. It details a detective's chase of a convicted serial killer that plays out in the Black Hills of Burkittsville in 1995 before the events of the film.

Other spin offs include a series of young adult novels that see Heather Donahue's fictional cousin investigating mysterious occurrences that could be related to the Blair Witch. *The Blair Witch Files* ran for eight books and further explored and developed the mythology with the final book in the series providing a thorough history of Elly Kedward from birth to curse. A comic book was also released to tie in with the film and was then followed by a four issue series entitled *The Blair Witch Chronicles*. For a tiny budget independent film, perhaps most surprising was the development of a trilogy of video games based around the film and in particular Rustin Parr, the events at Coffin Rock and Elly Kedward herself. Whether all these expansions of the mythology were cynical exercises in synergy or a genuine attempt to develop the story is open to debate but the mythology has certainly been exploited continuously.

Perhaps most cynical of all was the sequel *Book of Shadows: Blair Witch 2* (2000) that did little to enhance the legacy of the original film. Rushed into production, Artisan went ahead with the sequel despite the reluctance of Haxan. Myrick and Sánchez remained as executive producers but had little to do with the film. Joe Berlinger, director of genuine documentaries the *Paradise Lost* trilogy about real missing and murdered children, came on board but the film did not keep the found footage format from the original. Berlinger, Myrick and Sánchez along with critics and audiences have all expressed their disappointment with the sequel that featured a group of people investigating the Blair Witch and turning to murder, no doubt inspired by the curse. Myrick and Sánchez have since expressed interest in making a third Blair Witch film that will ignore *Book of Shadows* and may even feature Heather, Mike and Josh in some capacity.

Beyond this, however, the biggest legacy of *The Blair Witch Project* is undoubtedly the entire found footage sub-genre of modern horror. Though *Cannibal Holocaust* may have started the use of found footage in horror movies back in 1980 and *Paranormal Activity* made the genre more recently explode, it took the incredible success of *The Blair Witch Project* to inspire a whole generation of horror filmmakers to try their hand at the shaky-cam technique. Armed with tiny budgets and digital cameras, horror filmmakers from across the globe attempted to emulate the success of Myrick and Sánchez with varying degrees of success.

Some took the form of video diaries, some mock-documentaries, some home videos and some reality TV shows. Some made victims the stars and some made the killers the camera-carrying monsters. Many made a profit despite limited or straight to home entertainment releases due to their micro-budgets. Lacking big stars, expensive effects or even traditionally accepted aesthetics, found footage films started small and grew bigger and bigger and more common throughout the early 21st century.

It took until 2007 for the found footage phase to step up a gear and find itself firmly back in the mainstream. Oren Peli's *Paranormal Activity* was made for around $15,000 and then came to the attention of Steven Spielberg and DreamWorks who acquired the rights to the film thinking they would remake it on a bigger budget and release it. When the film sufficiently scared audiences at a test screening, a decision was made to release the original film and it went on to gross nearly $200 million at the global box office and to-date spawned three successful sequels. A year later found footage went (relatively) big budget with J.J. Abrams producing a Godzilla-style monster rampage through New York, all captured from a consumer camcorder wielded by a character stuck in the middle of the destruction. Inspired by YouTube videos of the 9/11 terrorist attacks of 2001, *Cloverfield* clearly still owes a debt to *Blair Witch* for its hectic aesthetics and limited perspective on a tragedy.

Found footage continues to be made with several very low budget films being released direct to DVD each year and also the occasional cinema release such as *The Last Exorcism* (2010) and the *Paranormal Activity* sequels. Found footage has even found its way into new genres with *Chronicle* (2012) tackling the superhero genre, *End of Watch* (2012) doing crime drama and *Project X* (2012) revelling in teen comedy. With low budgets and therefore minimum risk as well as the increasing acceptance of shaky-cam visuals and first person perspective videos on YouTube and even in news reports, the influence of *The Blair Witch Project* can still be felt far and wide.

The directors and stars have had less success with Daniel Myrick only directing a couple of straight to DVD features since and Eduardo Sánchez's career only picking up recently with *Lovely Molly* (2011) and his latest film returning to found footage in *Exists* (2014). Heather Donahue's career as an actress never hit the heights of *The Blair Witch Project* and she eventually quit acting to live on a farm growing cannabis and then write a book about her experiences entitled *Growgirl: How My Life After The Blair Witch Project Went to Pot*. Michael Williams has had infrequent TV roles and appeared in one of Daniel Myrick's later films, while Joshua Leonard has had steady acting work in film and TV.

With consistent rumours of another sequel to *The Blair Witch Project* and the return of the directors and stars a possibility, the legacy of the Blair Witch lives on. It is in every found footage film that exists and while the careers of the key cast and crew may not have fulfilled the potential of their breakthrough, horror has been significantly changed by this tiny little film, made in seven days in the woods.

REFERENCES

Cherry, B. (2009) *Horror*. London: Routledge

Denby, D. (1999) *The New Yorker* http://www.newyorker.com/arts/reviews/film/the_blair_witch_project

Edelstein, D. (1999) *Slate* http://www.slate.com/articles/arts/movies/1999/07/bare_bones.html

Franklin, G. (1999) *Dark Horizons* http://www.darkhorizons.com/reviews/109/the-blair-witch-project

Hornaday, A. (1999) *The Baltimore Sun*. http://articles.baltimoresun.com/1999-07-16/features/9907160262_1_blair-witch-project-daniel-myrick-wide-shut

IMDb http://www.imdb.com/title/tt0185937/

Internet World Stats http://www.internetworldstats.com/emarketing.htm

Richards, T. (1999) 'It's a kind of magic.' *Starburst*. Special (41), 68-7

Rotten Tomatoes http://www.rottentomatoes.com/m/blair_witch_project/

Schopp, A. (2004) 'Transgressing the safe space: Generation X horror in The Blair Witch Project and Scream' In: Higley, S. L. and J. A. Weinstock (eds) (2004) *Nothing That Is: Millennial Cinema and the Blair Witch Controversies*. Detroit: Wayne State University Press

Taylor, C. (1999) *Sight and Sound* http://old.bfi.org.uk/sightandsound/review/232

Telotte, J.P. (2004) 'The Blair Witch Project project: film and the internet' In: Higley, S. L. and J. A. Weinstock (eds) (2004) *Nothing That Is: Millennial Cinema and the Blair Witch Controversies*. Detroit: Wayne State University Press

Total Film http://www.totalfilm.com/reviews/cinema/the-blair-witch-project

Travers, P. (1999) *Rolling Stone Magazine* http://www.rollingstone.com/movies/reviews/the-blair-witch-project-19990730

Williams, M. http://www.youtube.com/watch?v=fWzMs9rbnAl

BIBLIOGRAPHY

Alexander, B. (2004) 'The Blair Witch Project: expulsion from adulthood and versions of the American Gothic' In: Higley, S. L. and J. A. Weinstock (eds) (2004) *Nothing That Is: Millennial Cinema and the Blair Witch Controversies.* Detroit: Wayne State University Press

Aloi, P. (2005) 'Beyond the Blair Witch: a new horror aesthetic?' In: King, G. (ed.) *The Spectacle of the Real: from Hollywood to reality TV and beyond.* Bristol: Intellect.

Anon. (1999) *Mythology: A Timeline of Major Events in the History of the Blair Witch.* http://www.blairwitch.com/mythology.html

Anon. (1999) 'An Exclusive Interview with Dan Myrick, Director of The Blair Witch Project.' *The House of Horror.* http://www.houseofhorrors.com/bwinterview.htm

Balasz, B. (1945) 'Filming Death' In: Macdonald, K. And Cousins M. (eds) *Imagining Reality.* London: Faber and Faber

Bergan, R. (2006) *Eyewitness Companions: Film.* London: Dorling Kindersley

Black, J. (2002) *The Reality Effect: film culture and the graphic imperative.* London: Routledge

Bordwell, D. and Thompson, K. (1993) *Film art: an introduction.* Palatino: Ruttle, Shaw & Wetherill, Inc.

Caro, M. (1999) 'Frightfully Frightfully, Frightfully Real: The Bewitching Story Behind The Blair Witch Project.' *Chicago Tribune.*

Carroll, N. (1990) *The Philosophy of Horror or Paradoxes of the Heart.* London: Routledge.

Castonguay, J. (2004) 'The political economy of the indie blockbuster: fandom, intermediality and The Blair Witch Project' In: Higley, S. L. and J. A. Weinstock (eds) (2004) *Nothing That Is: Millennial Cinema and the Blair Witch Controversies.* Detroit: Wayne State University Press

Cherry, B. (2009) *Horror.* London: Routledge

Denby, D. (1999) *The New Yorker* http://www.newyorker.com/arts/reviews/film/the_blair_witch_project

Edelstein, D. (1999) *Slate* http://www.slate.com/articles/arts/movies/1999/07/bare_bones.html

Franklin, G. (1999) *Dark Horizons* http://www.darkhorizons.com/reviews/109/the-blair-witch-project

Frappier, R. (2012) 'Interview: why are found footage movies so popular?' Available from: http://screenrant.com/popular-found-footage-movies-robf-154762/ [Accessed 14th November 2012]

Gallagher, S. (1999) 'Into the Woods.' *Filmmaker.* 7 (2), 72-74

Gaut, B. (1999) 'Identification and emotion in narrative film' In: Platinga, C. And Smith, G. (eds) *Passionate Views: film, cognition and emotion.* London: The John Hopkins University Press.

Grant, B. (2013) 'Digital anxiety and the new verité horror and sf film.' *Science Fiction Film and Television.* 6 (2), 153-175

Grodal, T. (1997) *Moving Pictures: a new theory of film genres, feelings, and cognition.* Oxford: Clarendon Press

Harris, M. (2001) 'The "Witchcraft" of Media Manipulation: Pamela and The Blair Witch Project.' *The Journal of Popular Culture.* 34 (4), 75-107

Hight, C. (2001) 'Mockumentary: Reflexivity, satire and a call to play.' Available from: http://www.waikato.ac.nz/film/mock-doc.shtml [Accessed 11th June 2013]

Higley, S. (2004) '"People just want to see something": art, death, and document in Blair Witch, The Last Broadcast, and Paradise Lost' In: Higley, S. L. and J. A. Weinstock (eds) (2004) *Nothing That Is: Millennial Cinema and the Blair Witch Controversies.* Detroit: Wayne State University Press

Higley, S. L. and J. A. Weinstock (eds) (2004) *Nothing That Is: Millennial Cinema and the Blair Witch Controversies.* Detroit: Wayne State University Press

Hills, M. (2005) *The Pleasures of Horror.* London: Continuum

Hornaday, A. (1999) *The Baltimore Sun.* http://articles.baltimoresun.com/1999-07-16/features/9907160262_1_blair-witch-project-daniel-myrick-wide-shut

IMDb http://www.imdb.com/title/tt0185937/

Ingle, Z. (2011) 'George A. Romero's Diary of the Dead and the rise of the Diegetic Camera in Recent Horror Films.' Ol3Media Available from: http://host.uniroma3.it/riviste/Ol3Media/Ingle.html

Internet World Stats http://www.internetworldstats.com/emarketing.htm

Kaufman, A. (1999) 'Season of the Witch.' *The Village Voice.* http://www.villagevoice.com/1999-07-13/news/season-of-the-witch/

Kendzior, S. (1999) 'How The Last Broadcast Came First.' *Fangoria.* 188 (1), 36-39

Klein, J. (1999) 'Interview: The Blair Witch Project.' *A.V. Club.* http://www.avclub.com/articles/the-blair-witch-project,13607/

Laycock, J. (2011) 'What If It's Real?: Live-record Horror and Popular Belief in the Supernatural.' Ol3Media Available from: http://host.uniroma3.it/riviste/Ol3Media/Laycock.html

Lim, D. (1999) 'Heather Donahue Casts a Spell.' *The Village Voice.* http://www.villagevoice.com/1999-07-13/news/heather-donahue-casts-a-spell/

Mannes, B (1999) 'Something Wicked.' *Salon.* http://www.salon.com/1999/07/13/witch_actor/

McDowell, S. D. (2001) 'Method filmmaking: an interview with Daniel Myrick, co-director of The Blair Witch Project.' *Journal of Film and Video,* 53:2/3, pp. 140-7

McEnery, P. (1999) '"Blair Witch" Heather Found Alive.' *Getting It.com.* http://www.gettingit.com/article/693

Metz, C. (1982) *The Imaginary Signifier: Psychoanalysis and the Cinema.* Bloomington: Indiana University Press

Moore, R. (1999) 'America's Scariest Home Videos.' *Starburst.* 255 (1), 52-58.

Neill, A. (1996) 'Empathy and (film) fiction' In: Bordwell, D. and Carroll, N. (eds) *Post-theory: reconstructing film studies.* London: The University of Wisconsin Press.

Nichols, B. (2001) *Introduction to Documentary.* Bloomington: Indiana University Press

Packham, C. (2012). 'The Rise of Found-Footage Horror.' Available from: http://www.villagevoice.com/2012-10-17/film/the-rise-of-found-footage-horror-paranormal-activity-4/. [Last accessed 23rd September 2013]

Pincus, A. (1999) 'Off the Beaten Track: The Blair Witch Project.' *The Independent*. http://www.independent-magazine.org/node/412

Poole, B. (2012) *Saw (Devil's Advocates)*. Leighton Buzzard: Auteur. 61-75

Pryor, T. (1947) 'Lady in the Lake (1946) At the Capitol.' Available from: http://movies.nytimes.com/movie/review?res=9C04E3DE123EEE3BBC4C51DFB766838C659EDE [Accessed 30th June 2012]

Richards, T. (1999) 'It's a kind of magic.' *Starburst*. Special (41), 68-7

Rotten Tomatoes http://www.rottentomatoes.com/m/blair_witch_project/

Schopp, A. (2004) 'Transgressing the safe space: Generation X horror in The Blair Witch Project and Scream' In: Higley, S. L. and J. A. Weinstock (eds) (2004) *Nothing That Is: Millennial Cinema and the Blair Witch Controversies*. Detroit: Wayne State University Press

Smith, M. (1995) *Engaging Characters: fiction, emotion and the cinema*. Oxford: Clarendon Press

Speigel, L. (2013) 'Spooky Number of Americans Believe in Ghosts.' *The Huffington Post*. http://www.huffingtonpost.com/2013/02/02/real-ghosts-americans-poll_n_2049485.html

Taylor, C. (1999) *Sight and Sound* http://old.bfi.org.uk/sightandsound/review/232

Telotte, J.P. (2004) 'The Blair Witch Project project: film and the internet' In: Higley, S. L. and J. A. Weinstock (eds) (2004) *Nothing That Is: Millennial Cinema and the Blair Witch Controversies*. Detroit: Wayne State University Press

The Blair Witch Project DVD Special Features

Total Film http://www.totalfilm.com/reviews/cinema/the-blair-witch-project

Travers, P. (1999) *Rolling Stone Magazine* http://www.rollingstone.com/movies/reviews/the-blair-witch-project-19990730

Tresca, D. (2011) 'Lying to Reveal the Truth: Horror Pseudo-Documentaries and the

Illusion of Reality.' Ol3Media Available from: http://host.uniroma3.it/riviste/Ol3Media/Tresca.html

West, A. (2005) 'Caught on tape: a legacy of low-tech reality' In: King, G. (ed.) *The Spectacle of the Real: from Hollywood to reality TV and beyond.* Bristol: Intellect.

Young, J. (2009) 'The Blair Witch Project 10 years later: Catching up with the directors of the horror sensation.' *Entertainment Weekly* http://popwatch.ew.com/2009/07/09/blair-witch/

DEVIL'S ADVOCATES

"Auteur Publishing's new Devil's Advocates critiques on individual titles offer bracingly fresh perspectives from passionate writers. The series will perfectly complement the BFI archive volumes." Christopher Fowler, Independent on Sunday

LET THE RIGHT ONE IN — ANNE BILLSON

"Anne Billson offers an accessible, lively but thoughtful take on the '80s-set Swedish vampire belter... a fun, stimulating exploration of a modern masterpiece." Empire

WITCHFINDER GENERAL — IAN COOPER

"I enjoyed it very much; it sets out all the various influences, both before and after the film, and indeed the essence of the film itself, very well indeed." Jonathan Rigby, author of English Gothic

SAW — BENJAMIN POOLE

"This is a great addition to a series of books that are starting to become compulsory for horror fans. It will also help you to appreciate just what an original and amazing experience the original SAW truly was." The Dark Side

THE TEXAS CHAIN SAW MASSACRE — JAMES ROSE

"[James Rose] find[s] new and unusual perspectives with which to address [the] censor-baiting material. Unsurprisingly, the effect... is to send the reader back to the films... watch the films, read these Devil's Advocate analyses of them." Crime Time

Printed and bound by CPI Group (UK) Ltd, Croydon, CR0 4YY

13/04/2025

14656601-0001